Introduction to Three-Dir
Principles, Processes, anc

Kimberly Elam

Princeton Architectural Press, New York

Published by
Princeton Architectural Press
202 Warren Street
Hudson, New York 12534
www.papress.com

ISBN 978-1-61689-921-9

Editor: Linda Lee
Designer: Kimberly Elam

Library of Congress Cataloging-in-Publication Data
available upon request.

Introduction to Three-Dimensional Design
Principles, Processes, and Projects

Table of Contents

The digital world tends to physically separate the artist and designer from their work with a glass screen. The only tactile sensations are the controlled tap on the keyboard, scroll and click of the mouse, or the stylus sliding across a smooth glass surface, resulting in the brain almost exclusively processing visual stimuli. The touch-driven three-dimensional world is far different. Tactile sensations ignite the brain, with about half of the brain's processing power devoted to touch. Within this process the hands are the workhorses of the sense of touch and are the most highly developed tactile receptors in the body, and when coupled with visual stimuli, energize the brain to become a creative neural powerhouse.

Imagine for a moment a sterile kindergarten classroom consisting only of blank walls and bland tables and chairs. This has to be imagined because all kindergarten classrooms are filled with colorful walls and arrays of paints, clay, crayons, blocks, and objects for children to touch. Everyone knows and teachers fully understand that engaging the sense of touch enhances and stimulates learning. When learning involves touch, it transforms the experience by deeply engaging the brain in a way that promotes the development of knowledge. This is a substantial cognitive link that goes far beyond rote recall or memorization.

The link between tactile sensation and learning does not diminish with age, and both adults and children benefit greatly from tactile learning. This is especially true of college art and design students, whose professions demand creativity. Tactile sensations not only stimulate the brain's processing power, they also enhance the creative thought, idea, or concept. Our brains are wired to work this way, and it is a primal impulse to doodle or craft or twist a paper clip.

My art and design college, Ringling College of Art and Design, is known not only for its excellence in art and design education but also as one of the most wired campuses in the world. (This is a good thing.) And at the same time, some of the most popular courses on campus involve touch-driven handcraft, including glassblowing, letterpress printing, sculpture, woodworking, book arts, printmaking, and serigraphy. Students intuitively crave tactile experiences not only as a welcome release from digital practice but also to get their creative juices flowing and enhance their problem-solving skills.

Introduction to Three-Dimensional Design collects a series of educational experiments that were conducted in my courses at the Ringling College of Art and Design. Almost all of the examples shown were designed, developed, and produced by freshmen design students in introductory three-dimensional design courses. These educational experiments are designed to tap into the benefits of tactile stimulation, and the students became my collaborators in testing ideas and developing the methodology. The approaches to the elements and principles of design are carefully crafted to focus on key concepts, from the initial sketches and experimental prototypes through to the final model solution. The dynamic forces of three-dimensional contrast are explored in the Mask project, with contrast employed as a means of intensifying communication of the contrast through juxtaposition. In Wire Icons, the continuous graphic line is transformed from two to three dimensions as the line becomes a wire that is sculpted to capture volume and space. Graphic communication and three-dimensional communication come together through abstraction in Paper Food, which enhances geometric box shapes with color and abstracted patterns to create iconic fruits, vegetables, and sandwiches. The Acrylic Bird project stimulates the imagination and challenges the student to reduce the ellipsoid body of a bird into a cohesive and recognizable series of clear planes. The objective with each three-dimensional project is to ignite the touch-driven brain and present the content in a way that thoroughly engages and enables artists and designers to deeply internalize, learn, and understand the elements and principles of three-dimensional design.

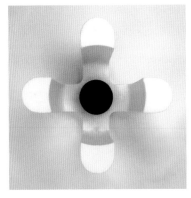

Radial Balance
Bella Cicci

Rhythm
Nicole Lavala

Harmony
Darien Kupec

Emphasis
Marcus Adkins

Proportion
Joel Reyes

Chapter 1. Principles of Three-Dimensional Design

Tho principles of three-dimensional design bring the elements of a design together. These principles are key concepts that describe methods of organizing, arranging, or juxtaposing three-dimensional elements with each other and to the composition as a whole. They are crucial visual forces that control the way the viewer interprets three-dimensional form.

There are many points of view as to what constitutes a definitive list of the principles of design. The principles that have been chosen for this project are those that are common and often the most visually powerful in three-dimensional design. These include proportion, scale, symmetric balance, asymmetric balance, radial balance, rhythm, emphasis, and harmony.

These principles are readily understood in theory; however, in practice they become more complex as visual forces combine and overlap. The most important goal of the project is clear communication of the principle.

Scale
Sophie Ruiz

Symmetric Balance
Tinny Hon

Asymmetric Balance
Elijah Adams

Project Process Overview

Research is empowering for the designer and enables a full understanding of the visual theory of and familiarity with the vocabulary associated with the principles of design and composition. Visual research includes examples (top row) from not just a single source but from a range of resources, such as nature, industrial design, and architecture. Each of these resources employs the principles in different ways and provides insights to the designer.

Next, the principles are visualized by drawing in two dimensions with the shape primitives of circle, triangle, and square with the computer (bottom row). This ensures an understanding of each of the principles and an ability to communicate the principle through drawing. Class critiques and discussions enhance this understanding and create a shared vocabulary of design. All work uses a square frame because it is a neutral format that focuses the viewer's attention on the interior elements and not the proportion of length to width of a rectangular format.

Research
Symmetry Principle

Symmetry in Nature · Symmetry in Man-Made Objects · Symmetry in Man-Made Objects · Symmetry in Architecture

Two-Dimensional Drawings
Symmetry Principle

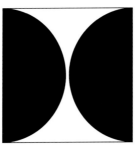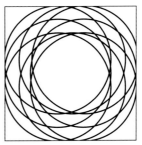

Mo Barrios · Foster Hirsch · Mo Barrios · Brian Zhao

After two-dimensional drawings, the principles were visualized with drawings that have the illusion of three-dimensions, with shade and shadow (top row). The extrude and revolve functions of software are used for this phase, and a sense of three-dimensional objects occupying space is developed. Experiments with composition begin to include an implied light source that creates shade and shadow.

Finally, three-dimensional models are created (bottom row) using simple materials such as Styrofoam, geometric solids, and wood blocks. What was easily understood and composed in the two-dimensional drawings becomes more complex and challenging, with consideration given to model orientation and camera angles. Similar to the drawings, all photographs are cropped into a square format.

Three-Dimensional Drawings
Symmetry Principle

  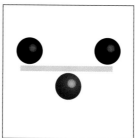 

Lok Yiu Louise Fung

Sophie Schonbach

Sofie Martin

Karlaina McClelland

Three-Dimensional Models
Symmetry Principle

Sam Grimm

Darien Kupec, Boram Kim

Katelyn Matikonis

Ally Jacobson

Color Constraints and Options

In this project series, work is done exclusively in a neutral square format for both drawings and photography. In order to simplify the project during the drawing phases, the use of color is limited to white, red, and black, including grays that are some percentage of black. This retains the focus on communication and avoids the complexities introduced by the interaction of color. Because of its brightness, red is frequently used as an accent to guide the viewer's eye. Red can also be used as a background. When any color fills the background, that color is neutralized and the focus is on the elements. The objective is that color is used purposefully to enhance communication.

Color Limitations
Even with limited color, there are many different combinations for this simple composition, especially considering the many grays that can be created from black. The examples (top and middle rows) show that the brightest color, red, becomes the most visually compelling color and can be use to guide the viewer's eye. Likewise, when white is used as a circle element on a solid color background (bottom row, left), it becomes the brightest color and hierarchically the most important. Filling the background of the format with any color, even red, tends to neutralize the background color.

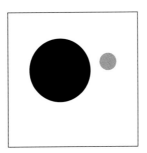 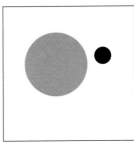 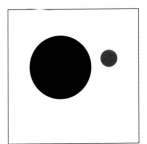

 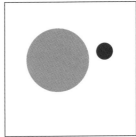 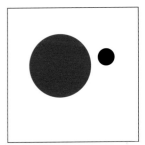

  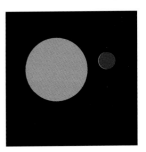

Tension, Relaxation, Cropping, and Closure

Visual relationships have meaning, and through composition that meaning is communicated. Tension is created in a composition when shapes are placed in close proximity to each other, near the format edge, or off balance. Close proximity creates a perceived sense of magnetic attraction, and the viewer's mind anticipates that attraction; off-balance positions create an anticipation of movement. Tension may be resolved and relaxed when shapes touch each other or when balance is restored.

The Gestalt principle of closure states that the viewer's mind has a tendency to complete incomplete forms that are cropped or hidden. This is especially true with geometric forms that are very familiar. The mind sees the fragment and automatically completes the shape. The use of cropping and closure enable the composition to become far more engaging not only because of closure but also the creation of the cropped element's relationship with the edge.

Tension and Relaxation

Shapes that are positioned near each other or the format edge create a tension of anticipated movement. When shapes touch each other or the edge of the format (top row, right), that tension relaxes when the elements are attached to each other, anchored to the frame edge, and at rest. Both compositions communicate the principle of scale, and the difference is in the tension or relaxation of the composition. Notice that the tension composition has a sense of anticipated magnetic attraction that makes it more dynamic and interesting.

There are many different ways to create tension in composition. The compositions with squares (middle row, left and middle) are filled with suspense as the viewer anticipates a fall, even though the square are simply ink on paper. Tension is resolved (middle row, right) when elements are balanced, relaxed, and at rest.

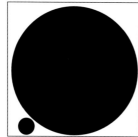

Tension

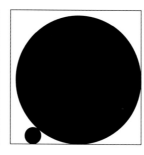

Relaxation

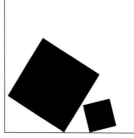

Tension

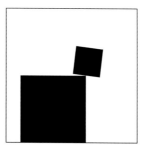

Tension

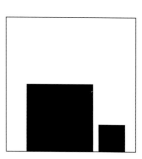

Relaxation

Cropping and Closure

Shapes that are cropped from the format frame are completed in the viewer's mind, creating closure as shown with the dashed red line. This often results in a more interesting composition due to the manner in which the shape touches the edge, which creates a ninety-degree angle in contrast to the circle. Cropped compositions appear to be larger as the principle of closure expands the elements in the viewer's mind.

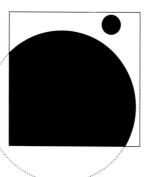

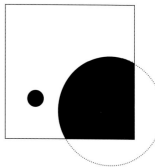

Depth Cues

Depth cues are a collection of visual concepts that enable the designer to create the illusion of depth and dimension through drawing. These cues have been used by artists and designers for centuries in order to create the perception of depth and dimension. An understanding of depth cues is essential in the creation of representations of the three-dimensional principles both in drawings and in models.

Scale change is one of the most familiar depth cues: objects closer to the viewer appear larger than those farther away. Since this project uses only nonobjective geometric shapes and solids, this relationship is described as a relative-size relationship. This means that since there is no representational point of reference, such as a person, chair, or building, the viewer makes judgments of scale based on comparison alone. Changes in scale can be enhanced through another depth cue called atmospheric perspective whereby more distant shapes are less saturated in color and the edges less distinct (top row). This depth cue mimics the haze in the air as in distant landscapes.

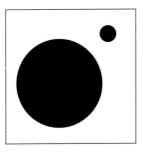 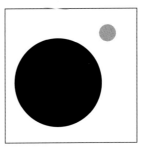 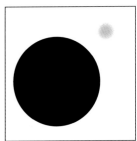

Scale Change
Scale change is a depth cue whereby the larger object appears closer to the viewer. Although both circles are black, the larger object is perceived as being closer.

Atmospheric Perspective
Scale change can be enhanced by changing the smaller circle to a less saturated version of the larger circle. This is the depth cue of atmospheric perspective whereby more distant

shapes become less saturated and the edges blurry. Note how much farther away the smaller circle appears due to a lighter gray color and soft blurry edges.

 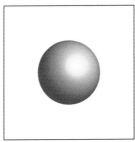  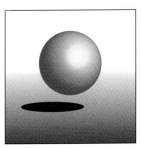

Flat
The gray circle is flat and without dimension.

Shade
Adding shading and an implied light source transforms the flat circle into a three-dimensional sphere.

Shade and Shadow
The addition of a shadow to the shaded sphere enhances the sense of a three-dimensional sphere because the shadow follows the three-dimensional shape.

Shade, Shadow, Environment
Finally, the use of the cast shadow makes the sphere appear to be floating above a surface, and the addition of a background gradient creates the illusion of a surface and environment.

Shade and shadow are depth cues that are essential in the depiction of three-dimensional objects (opposite page, bottom). They imply a light source that creates a range of tones and also highlights on the object. Shadows reveal clues as to the shape of the object and follow the angle of the light source.

Overlapping is a familiar depth cue whereby objects closer to the viewer overlap objects that are farther away. The sense of distance is increased by a color or texture change and may be still further enhanced by combining it with atmospheric perspective.

The depth cue of linear perspective is a system of drawing that mimics the way that the human eye sees: parallel lines converge to a vanishing point. Scale is a component of this system as objects recede in the distance to a vanishing point located on the horizon line. The horizon line and vanishing point are imaginary and determine the focal point of the viewer.

Overlapping
If there is no color or texture change, overlapping elements attach themselves to one another and become a single shape occupying two-dimensional space.

Overlapping and Color Change
When different in color, the two circles are distinct, and there is an illusion of depth and suggestion of three-dimensions since the two objects must occupy space in order to overlap.

Overlapping and Atmospheric Perspective
Three depth cues are at work in the example: scale change, overlapping, and atmospheric perspective. The small gray circle appears farther away as it becomes smaller, less saturated, and its edges softer.

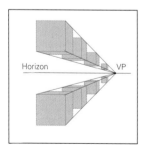

Linear Perspective
Linear perspective has three components: diminishing scale as objects recede in space, a horizon line, and a vanishing point (VP) at which all objects disappear.

Shade
Linear perspective is enhanced through the use of shade on the sides of the cubes, which implies a light source.

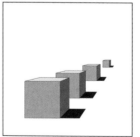

Shadow
The cast shadows further enhance the sense of space and follow the line of the edges of the cubes to the vanishing point.

Shade, Shadow, Environment
The gradient background creates an environment and surface for the shadows of the cubes as they recede in space.

Symmetry and Asymmetry Pairs

Those new to the study of design often struggle with the composition of and communication with nonrepresentational geometric elements. The notion of communicating with circles, triangles, and squares, which do not have any inherent meaning, is a foreign concept. In order to make the concepts more understandable, symmetry and asymmetry compositions are developed together as a pair. In other words, the same elements are used for both symmetry and asymmetry, with the only difference being the change in the arrangement of elements from symmetric to asymmetric. This practice invites comparison and enables a more full understanding of the principle.

Symmetric compositions are readily composed because of their strict formal rules of reflection. Most of these compositions are created with the axis in the center of the square format (top row). In both compositions, the invisible axis is made visible through the use of a vertical line, and this invites the viewer to experience symmetry and asymmetry in relationship to the axis.

Interestingly, symmetry and asymmetry are achieved with only one element, a wire frame torus (middle row). It is centered in the symmetric format, and through moving its position and cropping it from the edge of the frame, the figure and composition becomes asymmetric.

Elements can be symmetrically arranged along an invisible vertical axis (bottom row) but placed asymmetrically within the square format. The addition of the filled rounded rectangle shape balances the outlined figures and creates asymmetric balance.

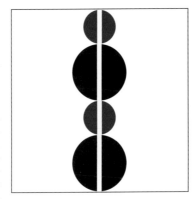

Symmetry
Faith Ruffin

Asymmetry

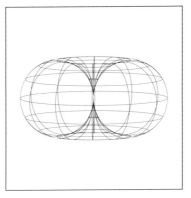

Symmetry
Aaron Kite

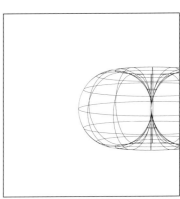

Asymmetry

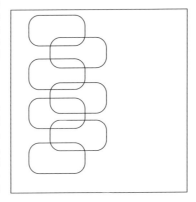

Symmetry
Sarah Hays

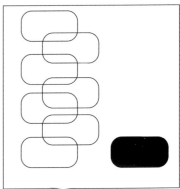

Asymmetry

Both of the models (top row) use exactly the same elements, but the orientation has changed from a front-corner view, where all objects align on a symmetric center axis, to a side view, whereby there is a distinct asymmetry. The change from symmetry to asymmetry is in the orientation.

In the middle row, both compositions consist of two cones and a sphere. Just as the circle is the most compelling two-dimensional element, the sphere is the most visually compelling three-dimensional element. Even though the cones point away from the spheres in both compositions, the eye remains riveted on the focal point, the sphere. The asymmetric composition points the cones in different directions, and yet the sphere remains the focus.

The simple structure of three cubes and two rectangular prisms in each frame (bottom row) shows the change from symmetric to asymmetric. The movement of one single cube from left to right makes the change.

Symmetry
Claire Capasso, Jordan Lilly

Asymmetry

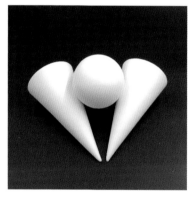

Symmetry
Olivia DeChant

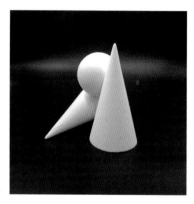

Asymmetry

Symmetry
Allyssa Ellis

Asymmetry

Model Building and Photography

With both the two-dimensional and three-dimensional drawings as inspiration, designers can test, evaluate, and photograph ideas for models very rapidly. Models are built with materials that invite quick exploration— such as foam sheets, wood blocks, and geometric solids. Skewers become the tool for connecting foam objects to each other and sticky poster putty connects wood blocks and foam geometric solids. Models are built, photographed, and then the materials are recycled for use in building the next model. Since work is done in a classroom setting, wood blocks and geometric solids cannot be cut. However, a hot-wire foam-cutting tool enables foam shapes and sheets to be easily altered and slabs of foam to be cleanly and accurately cut to size.

Drawings are a starting point for their models.

A hot-wire Styrofoam-cutting tool is used to easily and cleanly cut and trim Styrofoam shapes and sheets.

Bamboo food skewers are used to connect Styrofoam-model shapes.

Sticky poster putty is used to stabilize wood models.

In the classroom, a basic photography-studio setup of a black backdrop and two lights makes documentation efficient. Both digital SLR cameras and smartphone cameras provide good results. A stepladder is useful for capturing top-view shots. This simple backdrop and light setup enables ideas to be quickly tested, photographed from different viewpoints, evaluated, and, if necessary, photographed again.

Both digital SLR cameras and smartphone cameras work well when documenting models.

Choosing the best view for photography is critical when documenting models. The student uses a stepladder for an aerial point of view. A black background sweep and positionable lights help to make the photographs clean and professional.

The Principle of Scale

Scale indicates the overall size in relationship to environment, another object, or the human body. Scale is a comparison that informs as to the largeness or smallness of an object. When the viewer is familiar with an object, such as an office building or a sneaker, the comparison of the Big Blue Bear (right) or tiny plastic figure (bottom right) is startling. If photographed alone, without context, the miniature Eames Lounge Chair (below) could appear to be a full-size chair, but photographing the chair with the human hand, with context, gives the viewer the insight into the true scale.

The Big Blue Bear
The Big Blue Bear becomes a superscale sculpture as it is compared to the building and passing pedestrians. Lawrence Argent, artist

Eames Lounge Chair Comparison
Comparison of a miniature chair to the human hand

Tiny People Photograph
Cailey Ginn

Scale, Two-Dimensional Drawings

Visual interpretation of the principle of scale is enhanced by the use of similar objects because the use of like-shaped objects invites comparison of size rather than one of differences in shape or color (below, left and middle). When similar objects, such as circles, are compared, the communication of scale is clear and unmistakable. The inclusion of many elements (bottom, left and middle), often inhibits communication by creating complex interrelationships. The use of a limited number of elements frequently provides a clearer comparison of scale by focusing attention and inviting comparison.

The drawing phase enables the designer to develop an understanding of the principle by creating relationships between elements as well as experimenting with the compositional arrangement inside the square. As the designer's confidence builds, shapes begin to touch and are cropped by the edges of the format. Since these drawings are of two-dimensional shapes, the use of depth cues is limited, but the use of overlapping elements, cropping, and color change are irresistible.

Paula Rodriguez Ramirez

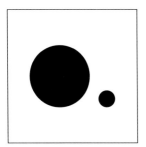 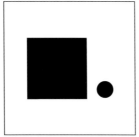

Comparison: Similar and Dissimilar Shapes
The use of similar shapes (above left), two circles, readily invites comparison for the principle of scale. Dissimilar shapes (above right), a square and circle, invite a comparison of shape rather than a comparison of scale.

Corrie Cubos

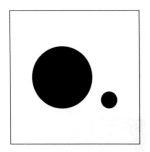 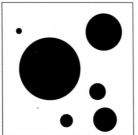

Comparison: Few and Many
The principle of scale requires a comparison, and the use of few rather than many elements. The example (above left) uses only two shapes, which readily invites the comparison. The example (above right) uses multiple shapes, which confuse communication as the viewer processes the many interrelationships of the elements.

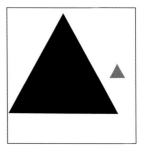

Aisha Vohra

19

Scale, Three-Dimensional Drawings

The three-dimensional drawing phase of the project employs compositional ideas similar to those of two-dimensional drawings, with the addition of depth cues. Shading of an object adds information about the three-dimensional form, and shadows enhance that information as they follow the contours of the surface.

Computer software can readily transform circles, triangles, squares, and rectangles into spheres, prisms, and cubes through extrusion or revolve. These software functions automatically create highlights and the illusion of dimension through shading. Cast shadows are added to enhance the sense of depth and dimension.

The objective is to clearly communicate scale change and these works are successful. This is because of the restrained use of only two elements, and the use of similar shapes which invites comparison of large to small.

Zia Perez De Jesus

Teresa Perez

Chloe Ward

Mira MacDonald

Drawings that crop one of the figures from the edges of the format (right) can be highly effective in the communication of scale due to closure. These examples are particularly successful in that the large element is cropped from two or three edges of the square, and the empty corners reveal additional clues as to the shape of the figure. Cropping changes the viewer's perception to make the elements seem much larger as the viewer's mind fills in and completes the cropped portions.

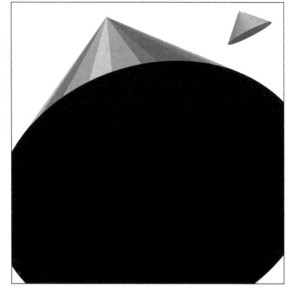

Bomsol Yoon

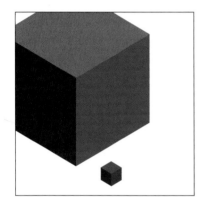

Tamara Marshall

Scott Rycroft

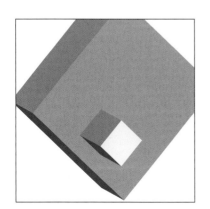

Mason Pocklington

Scale, Models

These compositions all use a change in position to communicate scale. The smaller element is placed far away in the background, making it seem even tinier in scale. The relationship of the objects is important; the point of view of the camera and the way that the composition is cropped in the square frame are also significant. Cropping of the photographed image in the frame (right) creates closure and enables the larger spheres to appear very large as they contrast dramatically with the small sphere in the background. The depth cue of atmospheric perspective is at work as the smaller spheres diminish even more through overlapping and blur.

Brooke Cardoza, Jamie Ohlstein, Roxee Zinsser

Shannon Davis

Gabriella Ozkosar-Perry

Mikey Pena

The problem of scale (right) could have easily been resolved by placing the large black cube structure and the small wooden cube side by side. Instead, the designer tucked the wood cube inside of the structure, making it feel even smaller. The change in color from black foam to wood grain and the cube's centered position in a symmetrical composition emphasize the wood cube as the focal point.

The bottom-row examples all benefit from tension and asymmetry. The overhanging wood cubes (below, left and middle) create tension as they are barely balanced in asymmetric compositions. The black cubes (below right) feel massive and create tension through the tenuous balance and compression of the centered small wood cube.

Danny Merino

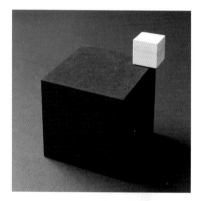

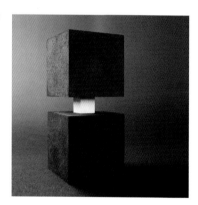

Lok Yiu Louise Fung

Sophie Ruiz

Ellie Winslow

The Principle of Proportion

Proportion is a comparative relationship of the relative size of a part or parts to a whole. Proportion is also related to ratios in that the relationship of the parts to the whole can often be expressed numerically: 1:2, 2:3, 3:4, etc.

Familiarity with the human body allow the viewer to immediately know when there is an extreme proportional change, such as the elongated arms of the sculpture (right). The freakishly long arms are unsettling and command attention. Anime artists change the proportion of the eyes to the face of characters so as to intensify the expression of emotion and to concentrate the viewer's attention on the eyes (below). The adult-sized and child-sized chairs (bottom) have a comparison relationship through the comparison of the larger adult chair to the two half-size child chairs.

Eye Proportions to Face

Human Body Proportions
Abyss, Emil Alzamora, sculptor

Chair Proportions by Comparison
Lou Lou Ghost and Louis Ghost
chairs by Philippe Starck, Kartell

Proportion, Two-Dimensional Drawings

Since proportion is a comparison of a part to the whole, the most direct communication is achieved by the subdivision of an object. When geometric shapes are subdivided regularly, the proportions are clear (below, far left, left, and right). The isolated square is one-ninth of the whole. The pie-shaped wedge is one-fourth of the circle. The white triangle is one-fourth of the whole. Irregular subdivisions (below, far right) communicate far less clearly, even though it is clear that the small circle to the large circle is a part to the whole.

The composition with squares (right) doesn't contain measurements but makes clear that the divisions and elements are proportional to each other. The two bottom examples show the proportional relationships through regular divisions, which enable the viewer to infer the proportions.

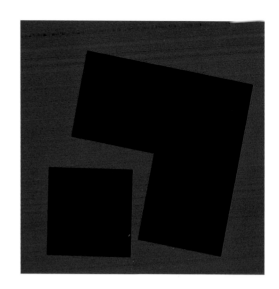

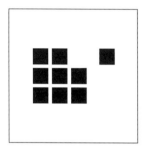

Square, Regularly Divided
1:9 Proportion

Circle, Regularly Divided
1:4 Proportion

Triangle, Regularly Divided
1:4 Proportion

Circle, Irregularly Divided
Irregular divisions create an unclear proportional relationship.

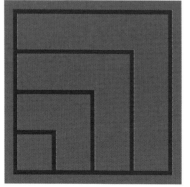

Caio Arias Nogueira

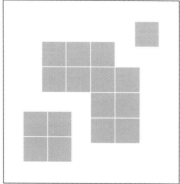

Sarah Hays

Proportion, Two-Dimensional Drawings

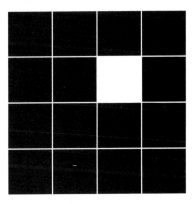

Adam Myerscough

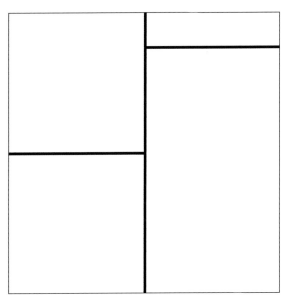

Jeremiah Dickson

The grid pattern (above) readily communicates the proportional relationship of the one white square in a pattern of sixteen squares, 1:16. The divided square (right) is less clear in its proportional relationships—the two squares at the left are each one-fourth, and the smaller rectangle at the right top has an inferred relationship of about one-eighth of the side or one-sixteenth of the whole.

The circle compositions (below) show three different ways of expressing proportion with circles. The black circle (left) shows readily understood pie wedges as one-half, one-fourth, and one-eighth of the whole. The red circle (middle) compares the proportional relationship of the diameters of the smaller gray circles, 3:6, and the larger gray circle, 1:2. The outlined red circles (right) show regular diameter proportions of one-fourth, one-half, and three-fourths.

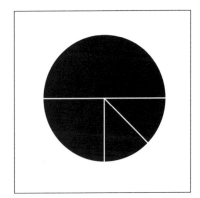

Jacob Garcia

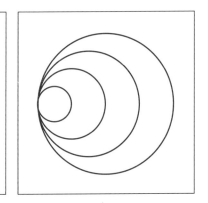

Tekla Khantadze

Taylor Stolz

Proportion, Three-Dimensional Drawings

Proportion requires both the part and the whole to communicate information. This comparison is most readily achieved with geometric solids that are regularly subdivided, such as the cube (right). The eye rapidly determines that the small cube is about one-eighth of the larger cube and fits into the void. Transparency is used to compare the edges of the cubes (below). The edge of the smallest cube is one-fourth that of the largest cube. Likewise, the edge of the next largest cube is about one-half of the largest.

The same is true of spheres and cylinders. The sphere and wedge (bottom left) communicate very clearly that the wedge is about one-fourth part of the whole. The cylinder has more ambiguous proportions, but it is clearly also a part of the whole.

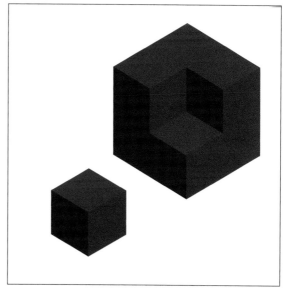

Ellie Zayas

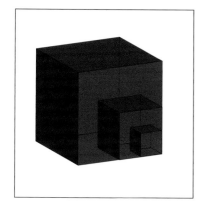

Olivia Dechant

Rebecca Miranda

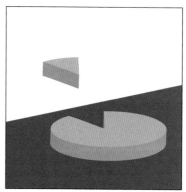

Erin Johnson

27

Proportion, Models

Some compositions create a visual comparison by massing similar objects, such as cubes or wood blocks, as a larger complete shape (right and below left). The change in color and position of the white cubes help to separate and emphasize the trait of a part of the whole. The prism structures (below right) are more complex objects with each structure consisting of two prisms and a cube. The single structure is compared to the combined structure of three.

The most direct way to communicate the principle of proportion is to subdivide a single element, such as with the spheres, green foam prism, and white foam cube in the bottom row. All four are foam shapes that have been cut so that a part is removed from the whole; or in the case of the white cube, the part of the whole is the inset small wood cube. The comparisons are explicit and evidence of proportional relationships.

Noah Jennings, Hyeonwoo Alex Cho

Bea Santos Patarata

Konrad Losiak

Rebecca Miranda

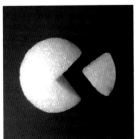

Sofie Martin

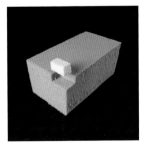

Eria Kozu, Soomin Park

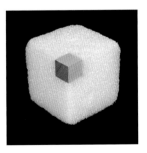

Bianca Lubrano

The relationship of the one-inch wood blocks to the two-inch blocks (right) is unmistakable. The single small cube nearest the viewer is clearly 1:8 or one part of the eight small cubes that make a two-inch cube. The composition conveys clearly, and the eye follows the center edges from foreground to background.

Massing of cubes clearly indicates proportion by separating part from the complete figure (below, left and middle). The proportions in the models are readily calculated at 1:4 and 1:8, respectively.

The idea of isolating one cube from a massed group (below right) is similar to the others, but the composition is different. The placement of the lone cube in the distance is far enough away to be affected by depth, resulting in the appearance of a diminished size that is framed by its own void.

Joel Reyes

Lok Yiu Louise Fung

Destiny Quezada

Petar Pirizovic

The Principle of Symmetric Balance

Symmetric balance is achieved when elements are arranged equidistantly (mirrored) on both sides of an axis with strict formal organization. Often, symmetry results in a pleasing composition as rapid visual interpretation, understanding, and acceptance of the composition is made possible. Most living things exhibit some form of symmetry, although in most cases it is imperfect when compared to man-made geometry. Notice that the arrangement of seeds in the kiwi fruit (below) is largely symmetric but not perfectly so, which is a tendency toward symmetry called approximate symmetry.

Man-made objects can be perfectly symmetric. The iPod (right) has a symmetric relationship in its click wheel to the screen to the rectangular case. Both the case and screen have rounded corners that relate to the click wheel and extend a harmonious and comfortable feeling to the iPod. The three-legged stool has legs that are equidistant to each other (below right). The position of the legs is both functional as well as aesthetic, and the leg joints are emphasized by the black color of the seat. The orientation of the stool in the photograph is symmetric.

Symmetric Controls
The symmetric placement of the control wheel within the radius rectangle speaks to the simplicity of both the product and interface. iPod, Apple

Cross Section of a Kiwi Fruit
Symmetry can be found in a multitude of growing things

Symmetric Orientation
The orientation of the stool in the photograph is beautifully symmetric, with each side mirroring the other. Icone Stool, Ashkan Heydari, designer

Symmetric Balance, Two-Dimensional Drawings

The composition below is in strict symmetry—the triangles can be mirrored left to right—and the symmetry is enhanced due to centered position of the triangles in the frame. Because there are no other contrasting visual forces, fully symmetric compositions are almost always less dynamic than their asymmetric counterparts. Changing the position of the elements within the square format (below right) from symmetric to asymmetric shift the proportion of negative space surrounding the elements, resulting in a more interesting composition.

Symmetry is relatively easy to create since the rules of reflection are strict. The composition with a circle and semicircles (bottom left) shows the left and right element mirroring each other. Even inventive experiments with symmetry on a diagonal axis (bottom right) reads as symmetric, with one side of the diagonal mirroring the other.

Symmetric Placement in the Square Format
John Beyea

Asymmetric Placement in the Square Format

Petar Pirizovic

Franki Coletti

One of the constraints of this project was to limit compositions to nonrepresentational elements. The mouse figure (right) stretches the boundaries of the project by creating a recognizable figure. However, the result is definitely abstract, truly symmetric, and rather delightful (so the rules were bent in this case).

The balanced seesaw (below) alludes to the physical balance of a plane on a fulcrum. Even though the elements have only the illusion of dimension, the viewer readily applies the rules of gravitational balance to the composition.

The vertical elements in the two compositions (bottom row) emphasize the symmetry of the spheres. In most instances, the vertical axis is implied by the viewer's mind, but in these compositions, the vertical axis is an actual element of the composition.

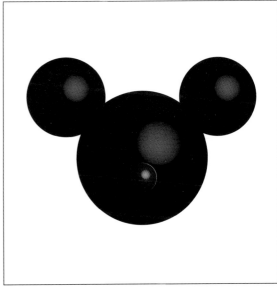

Jordan Lilly

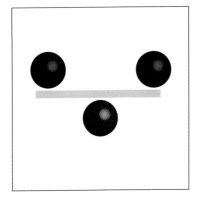

Sofie Martin

Faith Ruffin

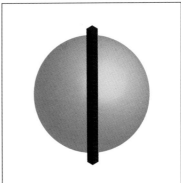

Karlaina McClelland

32

Cubes and other extruded or revolved figures depend on orientation to communicate symmetry. The three stacked cubes (right) are in an isometric arrangement, with the edges aligned and centered. The red cones (below) are symmetric because they are perfectly vertical. Likewise, the gray cones (below right) are symmetrically arranged with a red sphere floating above.

Spheres retain their symmetric qualities no matter what the orientation. The complex red figure (bottom) achieves symmetry because its axis is vertical and not pitched in space.

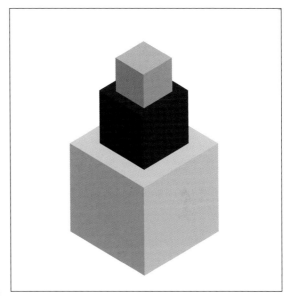

Sophie Schonbach

Sophie Schonbach

Paula Rodriguez Ramirez

Tekla Khantadze

Symmetric Balance, Models

Compositions that use regular geometric solids, such as the cones, cylinders, and spheres, on center (right) will result in a symmetric composition from many points of view as the model turns. The model of cubes and spheres (below) depends on orientation of the cube edge on center. Both of these models are symmetric. The negative space surrounding the model is also symmetric, as shown by the negative space examples (bottom, left and right) with a dotted centerline through the axes.

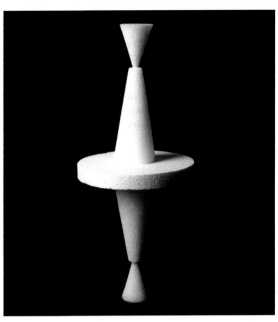

Symmetric Balance (above) and Negative Space (below)
Brooke Cardoza, Jamie Ohlstein, Roxee Zinsser

Symmetric Balance (above) and Negative Space (below)
Kathryn Klutes

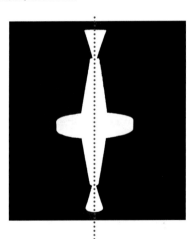

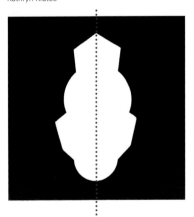

All of these models require a specific orientation for the strongest interpretation of symmetry because movement away from a specific point of view, by turning the model or altering the camera angle, results in an asymmetric composition. The designers worked consciously to make these models symmetric, with each side of the composition mirroring the other.

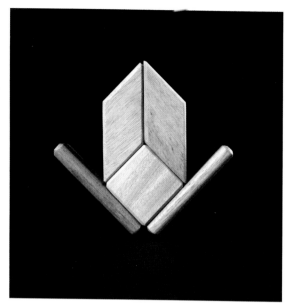

Martin Pohlmann

Claire Capasso, Jordan Lilly

Tinny Hon

The Principle of Asymmetric Balance

Asymmetric balance occurs when elements are not arranged equidistantly on both sides of an axis yet there is a sense of visual equilibrium or balance. This can be seen in the Table/Stool (right) in which the white vertical support is the asymmetric element. The cylinders of the seat and base reflect each other symmetrically, and the space in between the turned wood post and white support becomes the axis of visual balance. The same is true in the off-shoulder dress (below). The fabric is pulled over the right shoulder and balanced by the bare shoulder. The goal of the bonsai artist is to achieve a Zen state of asymmetric balance in the creation of living art (below right). The viewer imposes an axis on the asymmetrical tree, lending it a sense of beautiful visual balance.

Table/Stool
Carlo Contin for Subalterno1, Andrea Basile, photographer

Asymmetric Dress

Bonsai Tree

Asymmetric Balance, Two-Dimensional Drawings

Compositions that employ asymmetric balance are often more visually compelling than their symmetric counterparts due to the irregular placement of objects and slightly longer neural processing time required from the viewer. The reason for this is that the human brain seeks visual balance, and when it is not present, the brain imposes an invisible axis called a felt axis on the composition to make it so. The result is an intriguing visual puzzle for the mind to solve.

The outlined rounded rectangles (right) are placed on the left side in the format and are balanced by the solid black rectangle on the right. This results in a state of equilibrium and the felt axis is close to the center of the format. The imposition of an invisible felt axis occurs in all asymmetric composition, even those with a complex combination of elements, as shown in the two examples below.

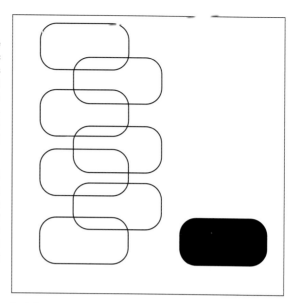

Sarah Hays

Felt Axis

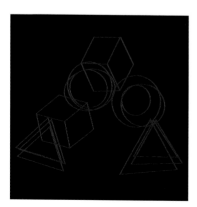

Anna Maksimenko

Felt Axis

Felt Axis

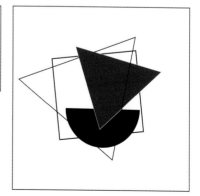

Anna Maksimenko

Asymmetric Balance, Three-Dimensional Drawings

The three-dimensional composition (right) uses placement of the axis as a compositional element, and the joining of the four spheres gives the composition a sense of balance. The stacked cubes composition (below right) requires the viewer to determine the placement of the felt axis to balance the offset cubes. The composition of the three tori (below top), are balanced by a change in color: the single bright-red torus balances the two gray tori. The two rectangular prisms (bottom) create a complex composition: they take different angles in space, with the axis occurring at the point where they overlap.

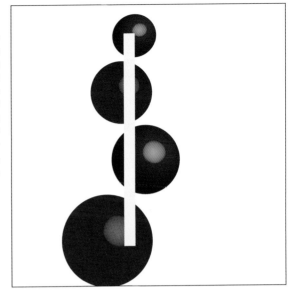

Faith Ruffin

Juliana Reolon Pereira

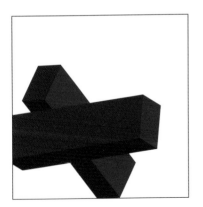

Yousaf Ejaz

Aisha Vohra

Asymmetric Balance, Models

Perhaps one of the most interesting aspects of asymmetric compositions is the irregular arrangement of negative space surrounding the objects. In symmetric arrangements this space is predictably mirrored, but in asymmetric arrangements it is irregular and far less predictable and therefore more intriguing to the eye, as shown by the negative space studies below.

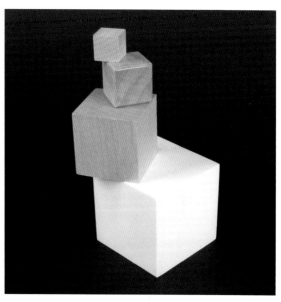

Asymmetric Balance (above) and Negative Space (below)
Aisha Vohra, Konrad Losiak

Asymmetric Balance (above) and Negative Space (below)
Jordyn Buckland

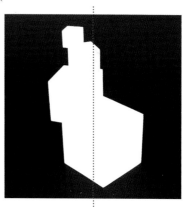

The space to the left and right of the felt axis is irregular and therefore more visually compelling.

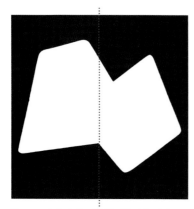

The space to the left and right of the felt axis is irregular and therefore more visually compelling.

The human eye craves balance in all things, and although the objects are arranged asymmetrically, there is a sense of balance in these compositions. The viewer's mind imposes the felt axis on the elements and establishes a sense of balance and order. The visual balance of the foam rectangular prisms (right) is also physical in that they rest upon one another. The slight movement of one wood cube (below) creates asymmetry; it also possesses the dual trait of asymmetry from the left and right and symmetry from the top and bottom. Even though the collage of the irregularly stacked solids (bottom) creates tension, the felt axis imposed by the viewer brings order and balance.

Ciara Lambert

Chloe Koonmen

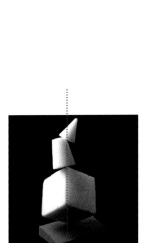

Felt Axis

Jose Lazarte, Alexa Masiello, Natalie Palumbo

The black sphere (right) is balanced between two rectangular prisms. The composition is asymmetric and achieves a sense of visual equilibrium that is enhanced by the cropped prisms. Likewise, the green cylindrical arc (below right) is balanced on a cube and a cylinder, which compels the eye to adjust and move the felt axis to the center of the arc. The sphere (below) is at rest between two cones and becomes the focal point between the two opposing directions of the diagonal and vertical cone points.

Elijah Adams

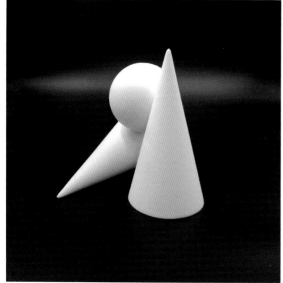

John Beyea

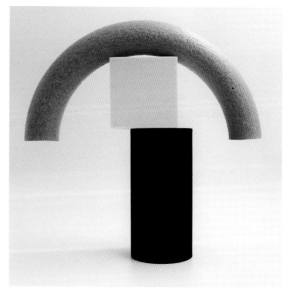

Nikhita Buddhiraju

The Principle of Radial Balance

Radial balance is a type of symmetry dependent on rotation around a center point and movement away from or toward the center. Most commonly, radial balance is envisioned as centrifugal whereby elements extend from the center, such as the spokes in a wheel (right), or concentric whereby elements dilate from the center in rings, such as rings of water (below). The spiral is a hybrid of the centrifugal and the concentric in that it both extends out and around the center as it does in the cross section of a cabbage (bottom).

Centrifugal Radial Structure

Concentric Radial Structure

Spiral Radial Structure

Radial Balance, Two-Dimensional Drawings

Most often, radial balance is visualized as a symmetric arrangement, but radial balance can also be asymmetric (right). In this drawing, the distribution of radiating lines is uneven, without fixed intervals, and the black circles are randomly sized and placed, giving the composition a sense of depth. The asymmetry is emphasized by the off-center placement in the square format, with an asymmetrically placed red circle that floats among the radiating lines.

Fixed centers and regular intervals result in symmetric structures (below), and centers that change position result in asymmetric structures that seem to swirl (bottom left). The spiral hybrid of the centrifugal and concentric structures (bottom right) both extends out and wraps around the center as the repeated circles enlarge, highlighting a sense of near and far.

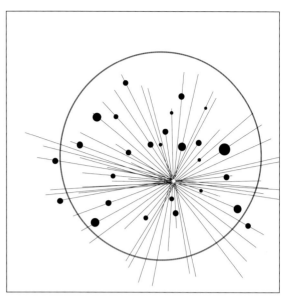

Asymmetric Centrifugal Structure
Anna Maksimenko

Centrifugal Structure
Jisoo Kim

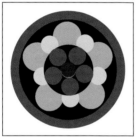

Centrifugal Structure
Kelsey Morris

Irregular (left) and Regular (right) Concentric Structure
Brooke Nilsson

Spiral Structure
Bianca Lubrano

Radial Balance, Three-Dimensional Drawings

Compositions with spheres (right) do not present problems with rotation because a sphere remains a sphere however rotated. The use of rectangular prism planes (below) does become more complex. Even though the point of view is offset, the composition still appears radial due to a center focal point and movement away from that point. The gray prism planes (bottom left) imply the existence of a center with the planes extending from the edge of an unseen figure.

Spiral structures are some of the most dynamic because they strongly imply movement. The gray spiral (bottom middle) is even more dynamic because it is a combination of three spirals nested together, which intensifies a sense of twirling movement with three arcs. The spiral of red cylinders (bottom right) moves into and out of the frame, which becomes a window into space.

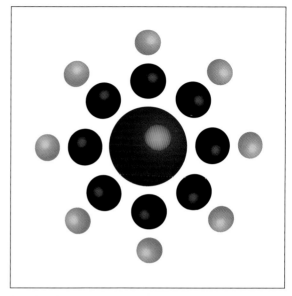

Centrifugal Structure
Rhiana Acuna De Leon

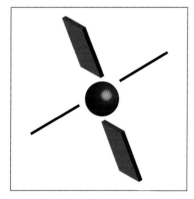

Centrifugal Structure
Kyjahana Irizarry

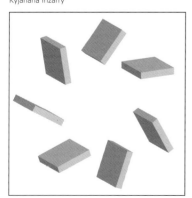

Centrifugal Structure
Ellie Zayas

Spiral Structure
Tekla Khantadze

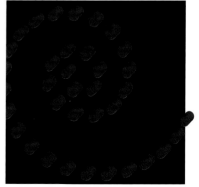

Spiral Structure
Bianca Lubrano

Radial Balance, Models

The square cube face (right) is a center point. Each edge of the cube has a tangent rectangular prism extending out from a corner and is a variation of the centrifugal structure. The same is true of other compositions that have centers that allude to geometric figures. The inside edges of the triangular prisms (below left) form a negative-space hexagon. A wood skewer also extends from an edge of each of the prisms. Each end of the eight rectangular wood prisms is a side of a hexagon (below right) and also an element that extend out from a side of the hexagon. In both cases, the eye is compelled to move either toward or away from the center.

Cones and elongated pyramids (bottom left) have tapered ends that serve as directional arrows to point toward and guide the eye toward the center, which is punctuated with a sphere focal point. The wooden cone composition (bottom right) employs negative space as the center focal point.

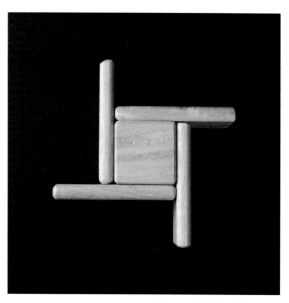

Centrifugal Structure
Corrie Cubos, Erin Lineberry

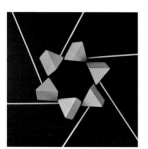

Centrifugal Structure
Aaron Kite, Stephan Carpenter

Centrifugal Structure
Olivia Dechant

Centrifugal Structure
Konrad Losiak

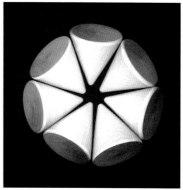

Centrifugal Structure
Ahmet Cevikel

Concentric Structure
Jisoo Kim

Concentric Structure
Tyler Abrams

Centrifugal Structure
Taylor Leitch

These compositions employ a circle or sphere as a center focal point. The circle is by far the most visually compelling geometric shape, and the eye is drawn toward it, making it almost impossible to focus on any other element when it is the focal point, even other circles. The focal-point circle also has the center position inside the square, the locus of attention, making it even more compelling. The other elements seem to recede and advance, but the eye always returns to the center.

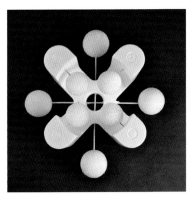

Centrifugal Structure
Michael Corey

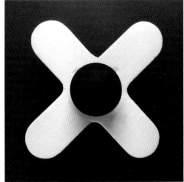

Centrifugal Structure
Mason Pocklington

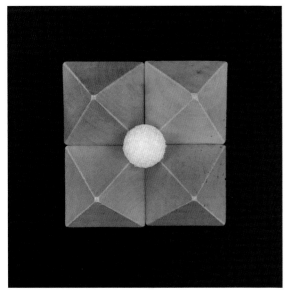

Centrifugal Structure
Chloe Koonmen

Centrifugal Structure
Kristen Molina, Jasmin Obedova

Spiral structures (right and below) invite the eye to follow the rotational arc toward or away from the center. The irregularity of the spiral cut from Styrofoam is appealing because of the changes in thickness of the material and therefore the negative space. The spiral made from differently sized spheres creates a sense of space as they appear to recede in space.

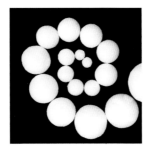

Spiral Structure
Kristen Molina

Spiral Structure
Jisoo Kim

The Principle of Rhythm

Visual rhythm is created through a sequenced repetition of elements that invite the viewer's eye to move. Elements can be organized according to a scheme, including repetition, progression, or random patterns. The most common form of visual rhythm is repetition: both the elements and intervals between them repeat either regularly or irregularly. The escalators (right) create a repetition rhythm of straight lines and curves. Progressive rhythms add gradual changes to the elements, such as changes in color, size, position, or interval. The classic peacock chair (below) uses a progressive rhythm in the back spindles that change size and direction. Random rhythms include groupings of similar elements with no regular intervals and are often found in nature, such as the bubbles on the surface of water (bottom right).

Repetition Rhythm
Paul Kilgour, photographer

Progressive Rhythm
Wegner PP550 Peacock Chair, Hans Wegner, designer

Random Rhythm
Yellowstone "S" Bubbles-Reflections in Yellowstone National Park, Wyoming, Rowan Nyman, photographer

Rhythm, Two-Dimensional Drawings

Repetition, progressive, and random rhythms can readily be made with graphic elements. The key quality in all three themes is that the arrangement causes the eye to move. These examples use closure and crop elements from the edge of the format, which causes the viewer to imagine the continuation of the rhythm pattern beyond the format edges. The random rhythms (top row) are informal rhythms whereby the different elements are similar and the intervals are irregularly organic. The repetition rhythms (middle row) have more of a sense of organization as the elements are repeated within similar intervals. Progressive rhythms (bottom row) have a gradual change in color, size, position, or interval that enhances the sense of movement by leading the eye.

Random Rhythm
Caroline Francoeur

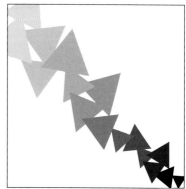

Random Rhythm
Nicole Constance

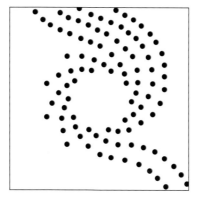

Repetition Rhythm
Anna Maksimenko

Repetition Rhythm
Miranda Williams

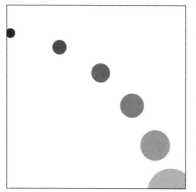

Progressive Rhythm
Ahmet Cevikel

Progressive Rhythm
Caleb Jacobson

Rhythm, Three-Dimensional Drawings

Many rhythms involving three dimensions are created through progression and are visually satisfying: the viewer's eye follows and anticipates the movements of the elements that occupy the space from background to foreground and/or foreground to background. The repeated cylinders (right) become even more engaging as the largest cylinder extends out of the square format, which changes the way the objects occupy space.

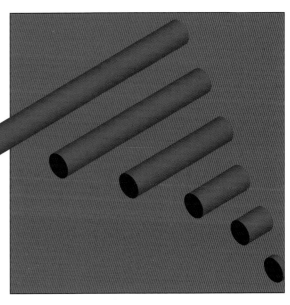

Progressive rhythms (below, bottom left, and bottom right) take advantage of space as the elements move. The stripes on the red sphere enable the viewer to understand that it is rotating as it falls, bounces, and recedes in space. Likewise, the cubes and cylinders in the other compositions turn in space and are affected by color changes as they move away from the viewer. The random rhythm (below far right) is a combination of circles and spheres that flow across the frame. Both the arrangement of the elements and the changes in color are random, yet as the scale of the circles and spheres increases, the pattern moves closer to the viewer in space.

Caleb Jacobson

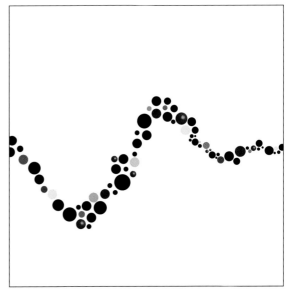

Petar Pirizovic

Rebecca Miranda

Erin Johnson

Rhythm, Models

The most dynamic rhythms are those that show repetition yet remain unpredictable, such as seen in the white foam cylinders (right). While the intervals are fixed, because the elements rest on each other, the lateral movements are irregular, which results in a series of fluid changes in position. The foam cones (below) have an irregular shape, which makes the repetition seem less predictable as they turn in space.

Designers are intrigued by the aspects of movement associated with rhythm and, for example, created movement through computer manipulation of cubes (below right) and wood spheres (bottom left). While digital manipulation is not within the project parameters, the experiments are interesting variations in the creation of three-dimensional rhythm.

Bria Jackson

Jose Lazarte, Alexa Masiello, Natalie Palumbo

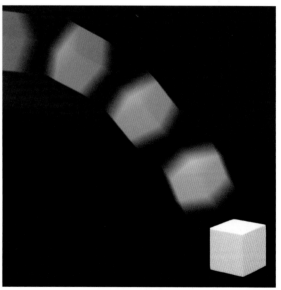

Caio Arias Nogueira, Bea Santos Patarata

Sarah Hays

Rhythms imply movement, and many models use predictable rhythms. This is especially true when the rhythm contains changes or intervals (right) that are consistent—a rhythm that can be described as an alternating ABAB. A regular rhythm can also be seen in the rotated and stacked arrangements (below left). The elements and intervals are regular but are made more interesting by the way the elements move and turn in space.

The cube and sphere arrangement (bottom right) begins with predictable changes in height but becomes more varied as the stacked cubes shift. The eye moves up diagonally and then shifts direction with the last two steps.

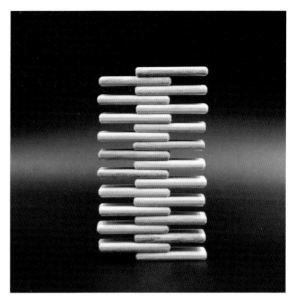

Danny Merino

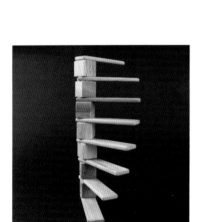

Petar Pirizovic

Ariel Taronij

Chloe Koonmen

The Principle of Emphasis

The design principle of emphasis is one of the most powerful visual forces designers can use. It can help the viewer readily recognize even a slight change in color, shape, or position, and these changes pull the eye to the point of visual interest. Emphasis is strongly related to contrast, and anomalies within a composition of similar elements, become visual magnets that compel attention. Emphasis is created when an element becomes a point of visual interest through the use of contrast, including contrasts in shape, color, dimension, or position.

The ability to see contrast and differences is hardwired into humans as the survival of our earliest ancestors depended on it: the ability aided them in tracking animals for food. Differences in compositional elements are also readily perceived by the human eye in much the same way. The raised three-dimensional red button (top right) contrasts with the other controls through color (red), shape (round), and dimension (raised). Isolation is also an effective emphasis strategy because it naturally attracts attention, as the paddleboarder (middle right) on the lake does. The use of color can, too, effectively direct the viewer's attention, for example, the red apple placed among the green ones (bottom right). The building facade (below) would be unremarkable if not for the hole punched through and the red and yellow structures with accent colors.

Emphasis by Contrast in Dimension, Shape, and Color

Emphasis by Isolation

Emphasis by Contrast in Color

Emphasis by Contrast in Shape and Color
Atlantis Condominium, Photography © Norman McGrath

Emphasis by Color, Two-Dimensional Drawings

Color is one of the most effective ways with which to create emphasis. It is particularly powerful in monochrome compositions that feature a single contrasting color element, as in the example (right) with the one tiny red circle. The project was constrained to the use of white, red, and black, and the most common color choice for an emphasis was red due to its brightness and because the inclusion of even very small quantities of a contrasting color can be compelling. The strategy also appears with a single black cube (bottom right), which stands out in contrast among the red wire-frame cubes.

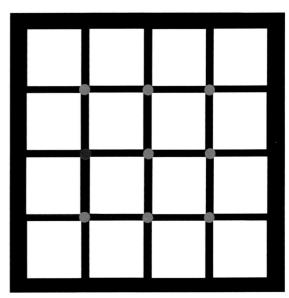

Bianca Lubrano

Miranda Williams

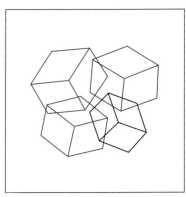

Juliana Reolon Pereira

Anna Maksimenko

Emphasis by Dimension, Two-Dimensional Drawings

Shifting from two dimensions to three dimensions through shade, shadow, and the suggestion of dimension is another method with which to create emphasis. The grid pattern of squares (right) is noticeably interrupted by a single shadow, which changes the gray square from two-dimensional to three-dimensional—an object must have dimension to be affected by a light source. Likewise, circles that are transformed into spheres (below and bottom left) contrast dramatically with flat elements, especially when they experience a color change. The flat red bar (bottom right) uses three emphasis strategies: it is the only two-dimensional element and the only red element, and occupies a position different from the other dimensional gray bars.

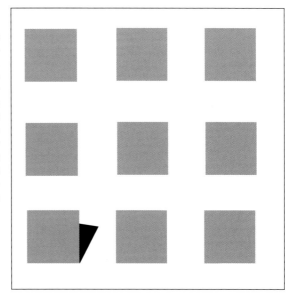

Stephanie Voinea

Aisha Vohra

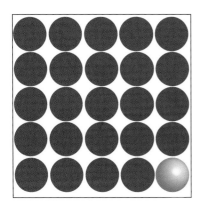

Lydia Wolfahrt

Bomsol Yoon

55

Emphasis by Shape, Two-Dimensional Drawings

Some of the most effective examples of emphasis employ more than one visual strategy. The composition on the right consists of regularly repeated black and white horizontal lines, but the contrast in color, overlapping position, and shape makes the thin red line the most dominant element.

Even without a distinct change in color (below, left and right), the emphasized shape still stands out and captures the viewer's attention. In these instances, the viewer's innate ability to distinguish differences is highly useful.

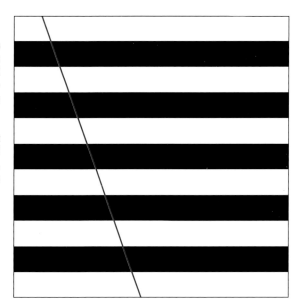

Emphasis by Position, Shape, and Color
Nicole Constance

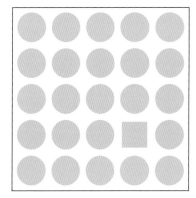

Hyeonwoo Alex Cho

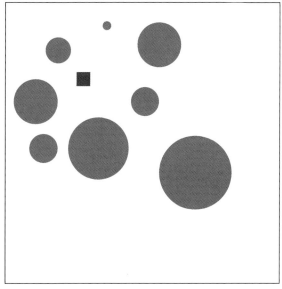

Mitchell Blass

Emphasis by Position, Two-Dimensional Drawings

Isolation (right) is an effective method to create emphasis. The viewer is captivated by the lone element as well as the negative space left in its absence. Similarly, the single absent cube (below right) compels attention, and in this instance, the emphasis element is the void created by the missing cube.

Moving or turning a single element in a grid pattern (below) creates irregularity in the midst of regularity, both with the lone turned square and the surrounding angled white space. The subtle change in shape from a square to a rounded square (bottom) abruptly changes the negative white space surrounding it, emphasizing the unique form.

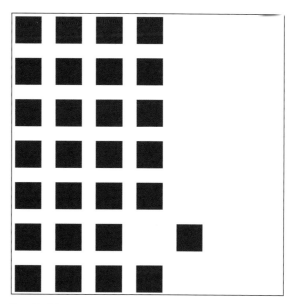

Konrad Losiak

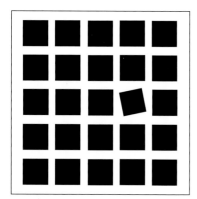

Petar Pirizovic

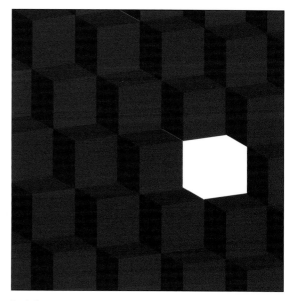

Sarah Hays

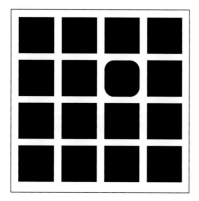

Sarah Hays

57

Emphasis, Models

In the regimented pattern of pyramid blocks (right), the tilt of one block from the pattern makes it prominent. The eye notes both the change in position and the shift in the shapes of the surrounding black background. Subtle differences in the shape of the pyramid among the cones (below) are easily identified due to the shadow along the edge. The sphere among cubes (bottom left) and cone among pyramids (bottom right) are more explicit and communicate the emphasis of a single element clearly.

Emphasis by Position
Chloe Harlan

Emphasis by Shape
Selina Bostic

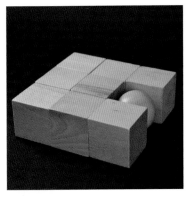

Emphasis by Shape
Hyeonwoo Alex Cho, Noah Jennings

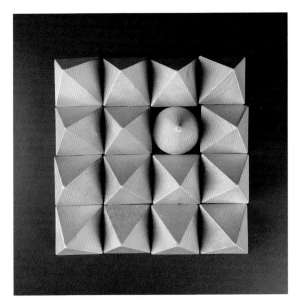

Emphasis by Shape
Bria Jackson

Many compositions use adjustments in color to empha-size a single element. The green Styrofoam sphere (right) seems to glow. The lone small orange cube (below) is nestled into the wood cube structure, with emphasis created by color and positioning. Even when the color change of the emphasis element is subtle (bottom), it can become a focal point. The most nuanced empha-sis composition here is the black cube among white spheres (below right). Since the cube color is the same as the background, the cube can only be identified by the contrast of straight edges against the white spheres.

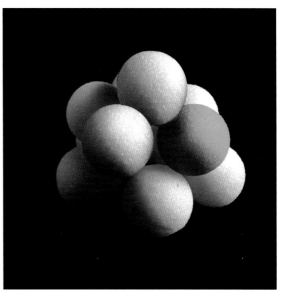

Emphasis by Color
Brooke Cardoza, Jamie Ohlstein, Roxee Zinsser

Emphasis by Color
Olivia Dechant

Emphasis by Shape and Color
Iana Prakheeva

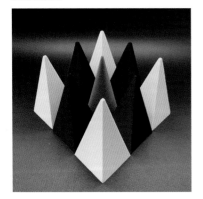

Emphasis by Shape and Color
Marcus Adkins

The Principle of Harmony

Harmony exists when all parts of the design relate to and complement each other, and the viewer senses that the elements belong together, without the presence of stress or tension. Often, harmonious compositions are symmetric and have a visual language of repeated, related elements or shapes. The use of a consistent visual language can be seen in the elliptical shape of the stones (right), which are comfortably at rest. Birds weave twigs in an organic bowl (below left) to make a nest for eggs. The abstract and repeated interlocking ceramic forms (below right) all seem to belong to each other.

Harmony in Stacked Stones

Harmony in Twig Shapes

Harmony in Interlocking Ceramic Forms
Black Loop, Merete Rasmussen, sculptor

Harmony, Two-Dimensional Drawings

The yin-yang symbol symbolizes perfect harmony, a balance between positive and negative forces, which are enclosed by a circle representing the universe. There is a sense of fluid movement of two forces that balance and complement each other.

Harmony within geometric elements suggests that the composition and the elements are balanced. Elements that share a visual language often have a harmonious relationship. Symmetric compositions often achieve this balance; simplicity minimizes the interaction of elements and affirms this equilibrium.

Yin Yang Symbol

Olivia Dechant

Lauren Cash

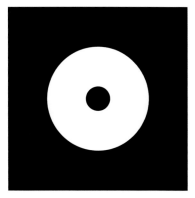

Chloe Ward

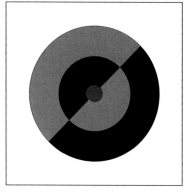

Juliana Reolon Pereira

Harmony, Three-Dimensional Drawings

Without representational images, the idea of harmony is elusive and subjective. The limited number of geometric shapes and solids means that they rely on symmetric balance and on forms that echo each other with a sense of belonging.

Even though the hemisphere and cube (right) do not share a shape language, the comfortable manner in which they rest together suggests harmony. Interestingly, a similar composition of wood solids (opposite page, left) feels even more harmonious because the close relationship between the material and color. The examples all are symmetric, with elements at rest.

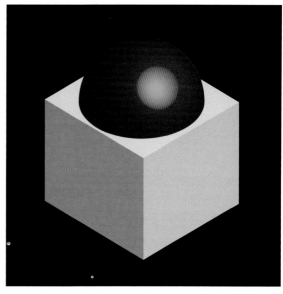

Scott Rycroft

Sofie Martin

Caleb Jacobson

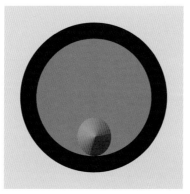

Erin Johnson

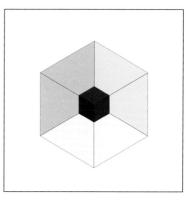

Olivia Dechant

Harmony, Models

The wood block shapes (right) seem to hug each other with the flat surfaces of parallelogram prisms. The eye moves across the square and rectangular surfaces of one edge to the next, with lines converging at the center. All of the models on this page share the sense that the shapes belong together and are at rest without stress or tension. Even when the shapes are dissimilar, as in the cube and hemisphere (below), the use of the same material, wood, plus a comfortable relationship, the fit of the sphere on the cube, makes the result harmonious. The cube and parallelogram prisms (bottom) unexpectedly share angles and come together as a whole.

Darien Kupec

Olivia Dechant, Scott Rycroft

Caroline Francoeur, Brooke Nilsson

The model (right) consists of a sphere resting inside a hollow hemisphere. Even though the color is different, the two elements share the same shape language and because of this, the symmetry of the composition, and the nesting, the two elements appear as if they belong together. The wood cubes (below) and parallelogram prisms (bottom right) use repeated shapes in a single symmetric structure. Even the cone spiral (bottom left) is a single shape.

Brooke Cardoza, Jamie Ohlstein, Roxee Zinsser

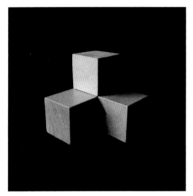

Anna Maksimenko

Kyle Leight, Vanessa Bundschu

Hyeonwoo Alex Cho

While the model at right does not have elements that share a shape language, the stark symmetry of the composition and resting positions of the sphere supported by the cones communicates a harmonious arrangement. Each of the other three models below consist of similar shapes that come together to form a single structure. The three pyramids (below), two upright and one inverted, come together and share angles. The repeated stacked wood rectangular prisms (bottom left) are regularly arranged and approach symmetry. The stacked small wood cubes (bottom right) nestle together as a large cube without tension.

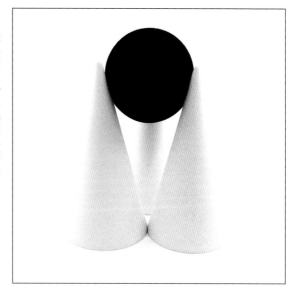

Duncan Demichiel

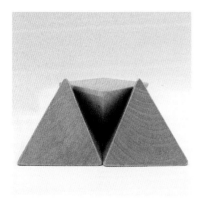

Zaine Lodhi

Rhiana Acuna De Leon

Brian Zhao

Positive to Negative
Stephen Moore

Concave to Convex
Mackenzie Schlagenhaft

Geometric to Organic
Kelsey Morris

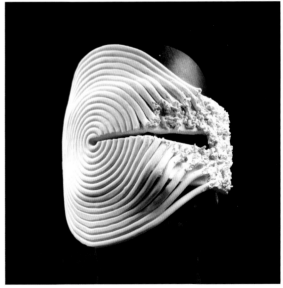

Smooth to Rough
Matthew Lupo

Tension to Relaxation
Michiru Morita

Chapter 2. Three-Dimensional Contrasts, Mask Design

Design students often struggle as they leave the familiar environment of iconic images and enter the abstract world of nonrepresentational imagery. This world consists of geometric and organic shapes that in themselves do not have meaning. It is by conscious form making, juxtaposition, and composition that contrast is created. The resulting work is subtle and nuanced in that it relies on the dimensional interplay of form and light to reveal the contrast.

Frequently, explorations of the principles of art and design are conducted only as theoretical exercises. This project brings life to three-dimensional contrasts and makes the composition of those contrasts an exciting exploration resulting in the production of a stunning mask. These contrasts are the universal visual language of art and design that inspire and guide creativity in unexpected ways. The masks are both functional and aesthetic—they are wearable sculptures.

It would be impossible to generate a definitive list of all three-dimensional contrasts—those that have been chosen for this project are common and suitable for polymer clay. The contrasts can be thought of as opposites, and those opposites are brought together in a singular form, with each student bringing his or her own ideas, sensibilities, and interpretations.

Economy to Intricacy
Darien Kupec

Expected to Unexpected
Hyeonwoo Alex Cho

Geometric to Organic
Stephen Moore

Project Process Overview

The subject of a mask was chosen for this project because a mask embodies both functional and aesthetic qualities. Additionally, the subject of a mask could readily combine problem-solving with three-dimensional composition, bringing visual theory to practice and making students enthusiastic learners. The mask is a familiar form to design students and are often symbolic of the superhero or an alter ego. Historically, some of the most beautiful masks were created by ancient and indigenous people as spiritual and ceremonial expressions of their power, mysticism, and dreams (below right).

There is a wealth of visual research regarding masks through online resources. Contemporary fashion designers produce masks (below left) as fashion accessories and combine new materials and ideas, while others explore sculptural qualities (below middle).

Tile design, which has traditionally consisted of flat geometric shapes, is undergoing a renaissance of three-dimensional form as designers experiment with relief textures that result in beautiful patterns of shade and shadow.

Research

White Drop Mask
2010; brass, resin, leather; Midnight Dance Collection; Joji Kojima, designer; Mika Kamakura, model

M05 Geometric Mask
Erick Roinestad, ceramic artist

Mask: Face of a Tungak?
Late-nineteenth century; wood and paint, 7 3/8 x 6 1/2 in. (18.73 x 16.51 cm.); Dallas Museum of Art, gift of Elizabeth H. Penn, 1982.82

Bentu Six 1 Wall Tiles, Öopenspace
Interior installation of tiles showing the effects of shade and shadow

Bentu San Wall Tiles, Öopenspace
Interior installation of tiles showing the effects of shade and shadow

The list of three-dimensional contrasts was developed to prompt visual ideas and possibilities that range from the extreme to the more nuanced and subtle. Within these possibilities is a wide range of potential for visual expression, insight, and understanding. Visual ideas come together through and with personal interpretation, media, and composition to achieve the goal of visual communication of contrast.

Before designing a mask, an understanding of the three-dimensional contrasts and experience with modeling polymer clay are necessary. This can be accomplished by making a series of small, four-inch-square, relief tile compositions to test visual ideas and to develop craft techniques. It is through these experimental compositions that designers learn how to craft the material and freely experiment with creative ideas.

Contrast List

Concave to Convex

Dominant to Subordinate

Economy to Intricacy

Expected to Unexpected

Flat to Folded

Geometric to Organic

Positive to Negative

Rhythm to Variation

Small to Large

Smooth to Rough

Static to Active

Symmetry to Asymmetry

Tension to Relaxation

Polymer Clay Tile Experiments

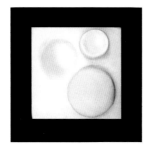

Concave to Convex

Dominant to Subordinate

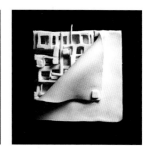

Economy to Intricacy

Flat to Folded

Geometric to Organic

Positive to Negative

Rhythm to Variation

Smooth to Rough

Tension to Relaxation

A mask template is provided as a guide and a starting point. The mask template is based on the harmonious proportions of a module of three inches with all measurements based on that module of proportional relationships. The rectangle is three inches by nine inches, with the eye openings along the horizontal centerline at three inches apart. The dimensions and shape of the mask could be altered depending on the mask concept, but, at minimum, one eye opening of any shape needed to remain.

The theme of each mask is based on one of the three-dimensional contrasts, and the tile experiments were the inspiration for designs. Drawings show the contrast theme and the functional eye openings, and the drawing became the plan for the crafting of the final mask in polymer clay. The final mask design often underwent changes as ideas and technical considerations evolved.

Mask Drawing Template

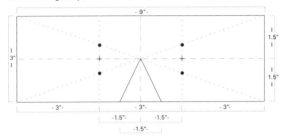

Mask Drawings

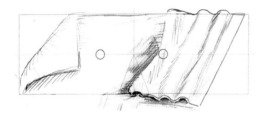

Flat to Folded Drawing
Teresa Perez

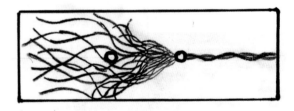

Tension to Relaxation Drawing
Teresa Perez

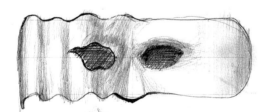

Flat to Folded Drawing
Joseph Woods

Tension to Relaxation Drawing
Taylor Leitch

Sometimes the final clay mask can be directly traced from an experimental tile to the mask drawing and finally to the modeled mask. In these instances, the tile, drawing experiences, and clay modeling directly built on each other. In other instances, the design process is less direct and the drawings and final mask bear little resemblance to the tiles. These masks express fresh ideas that involve curiosity regarding other contrasts, research, and skill in crafting techniques, and inspiration from research and tile experiments, all which influenced the design of the final mask. Both pathways to the final result yield excellent results and are valid—the design process and creativity are often unpredictable.

Masks

Dominant to Subordinate

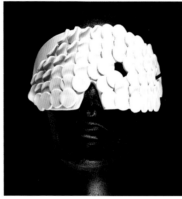

Flat to Folded

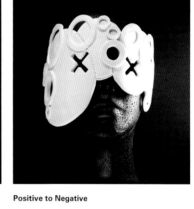

Positive to Negative

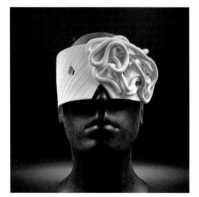

Static to Active

Tension to Relaxation

Small to Large

Oven-bake polymer clay is soft, and unsupported masks will not hold their shape. A U-shaped metal form holds the mask when it is being crafted and modeled and then when baked in an oven to ensure that it will curve around the face when worn. This form is made from an inexpensive roll of roof-flashing aluminum and secured with strips of bent aluminum. A triangle of aluminum is cut with metal shears and bent to shape the nosepiece. Very thick solid clay pieces, such as large spheres, will likely crack; therefore, large shapes on the masks are made with crumpled aluminum foil core and covered with a thin layer of clay. Baking clay on the form solidifies the mask into a strong and permanent shape.

Aluminum-Form Support

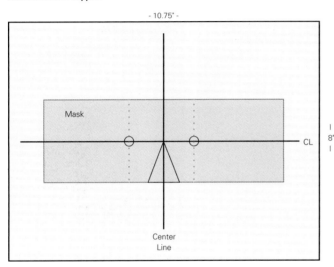

The aluminum form is 10.75" x 8" and is cut from a roll of aluminum roof flashing. It is important to cut the aluminum sheet squarely to create a symmetrical bend. Center lines are drawn on the form with a permanent fine line marker in order to keep the mask centered and evenly bent from the nose.

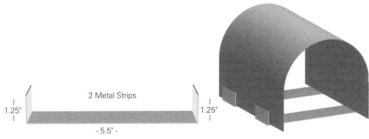

Aluminum Strips
Two or more aluminum strips keep the aluminum form bent during crafting and baking. These strips can be secured with clamps or masking tape.

Polymer clay is available in original and ultralight versions. Original polymer clay is dense, heavy, and can be quite stiff, but it can be softened with Liquid Clay Softener. Its advantage is that it holds its shape well, especially with delicate details. The disadvantage is that it is heavy for a mask that is intended to be worn.

Ultralight clay is just that—extremely lightweight. It is softer and easier to work but can be too soft for crisp details. This can be remedied by sandwiching a clay slab between two pieces of paper overnight, which slightly dries the clay and stiffens it. A mask made of baked ultralight clay can easily and comfortably be worn.

Rolling and Cutting Clay

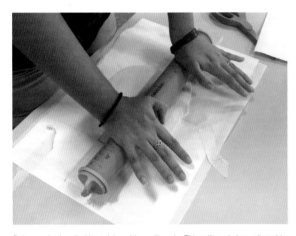

Polymer clay is rolled into slabs with a rolling pin. This rolling pin has adjustable thickness guides for rolling a uniform slab. Parchment baking paper keeps the clay from sticking to the table surface.

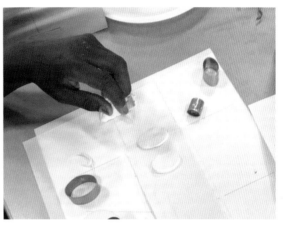

Cookie cutters, especially sets of geometric cutters, are useful for cutting uniform shapes. Small punch cutters, used for cake decoration, are also excellent for cutting clay.

Clay-extrusion tools create long uniform shapes such as these clay "noodles" as well as a variety of ribbonlike shapes.

A pasta roller helps create very thin sheets of polymer clay, which are difficult to roll by hand.

Concave to Convex Contrast

Concave surfaces bulge inward as would a depression in a flat surface, and convex surfaces bulge outward as would a hill or the lens of a magnifying glass. The concave to convex contrast is similar to the positive to negative contrasts, but it is often more nuanced, with slighter changes in the surface. The changes in dimension can be minimal and subtle, with the elevation or depression of the surface communicated with shade and shadow. Geometry can be used to create crisper raised surfaces or voids, which can be interpreted as concave or convex spaces.

The example at right employs both a crisp geometric edge on the outer circle rings and soft indented technique. The concentric rings build up to create the convex surfaces, and the gradual gentle dent in the center is the concave area.

The minimal composition (below left) contrasts the concave depression with a sphere-like convex element. The two other examples below experiment with the square format. A soft convex circle (below middle) overlaps the lower-right corner in contrast to the opposite corner, which is concave and has a cropped corner. Additionally, smaller concave depressions and two convex spheres provide visual interest. A similar strategy is used (below right) to shape the square with convex circles that overlap the edges and are in counterpoint to the concave depressions and the geometric void at the top.

Mask and Tile Models

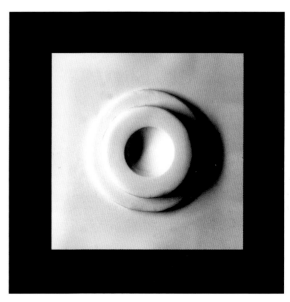

Martin Pohlmann

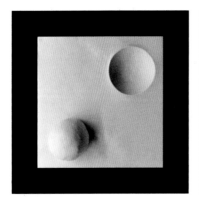

Emily Griffith

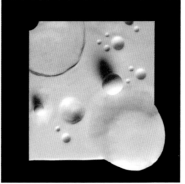

Teresa Perez

Luke Tiday

The single eye opening of this mask (right) accentuates the asymmetry of the composition. The right side is highly active, with multiple circle rings denoting convex space. The left side is simpler, with only two rings. The eye opening creates an asymmetric balance between the two sides.

Bianca Lubrano

Dominant to Subordinate Contrast

Dominance is closely related to the design principle of emphasis in that when any element of a design becomes a focal point it becomes the dominant component. In three-dimensional design, common methods employed to create dominance are through manipulation of other contrasts, such as those in scale—large dominates small—and position—top dominates bottom.

In the composition of extruded ribbonlike elements (right), the dominant element is the single horizontal line that seems to pin down the vertical extruded lines. It is almost as if the twists and turns in the lines depict a futile struggle to break free.

Scale allows the large slab (below left) to dominate by overlapping the small square. Likewise, the large negative-space triangle (below middle) becomes a focal point due to the scale and by being a void that reveals the black background. The top position of the three raised circles (below right) readily dominates the repeated incised circles with dimensionality and overlapping.

Jingyun Zhou

Sam Grimm

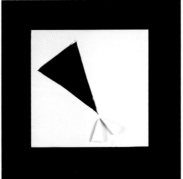

Sophia Holland

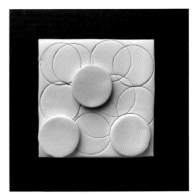

Chloe Harlan

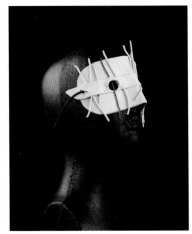

Similar to the four-inch experiment (opposite page, top), the horizontal band holds the vertical extruded lines in place (above and right). In addition, a lone black-wire line dominates because of the change in color and the interruption of the eye circle. Black wire is also used (below) as a dominant element to contain and control the nose and eye openings as if to dominate the senses.

Jingyun Zhou

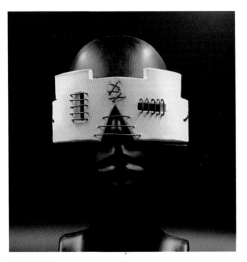

Maddy Mcelwee

Economy to Intricacy Contrast

Economy is the sparing and judicious arrangement of elements whereas intricacy is lavish and excessive. This contrast can also be described as one between simplicity and complexity.

The work at right contrasts a single extruded horizontal line with a tangle of lines, clearly communicating economy and intricacy. Interestingly, a curvilinear line moves from of the tangle toward the single line, which attracts the viewer's eye and connects the two elements. A tangle is also used to portray complexity (right) with the fine noodle-like lines melting into the smooth slab to exemplify simplicity.

The ordered and repeated grid pattern (below left) is interrupted by tenuous lines that intertwine and disrupt the regularity of the grid. The horizontal and vertical ordered regularity is economy in contrast to the disorder of the intertwining curves. The diamond grid pattern (below right) shows a transformation from an empty grid square at the bottom to progressively more embellished grid squares—economy and intricacy.

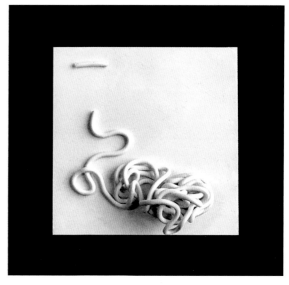

Rebecca Miranda

Darien Kupec

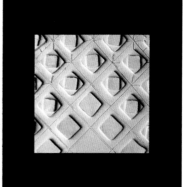

Ellie Winslow

78

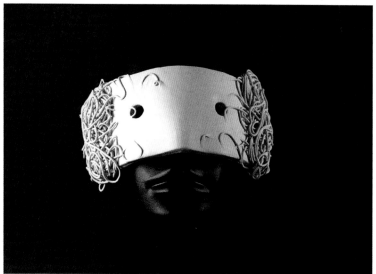

Teresa Perez

The mask above was strongly inspired by the four-inch tile experiment (opposite page, bottom left). The tangle of extruded lines moves away from the center. Wisps of lines interact with the eye openings and almost melt into a smooth liquid surface. The mask (left and below) also uses a tangled mass to communicate intricacy. The tangle is tightly clustered on one side and wraps around the edges and into the eye opening. A crack in the clay slab above the nose separates the economic side from the intricate side, creating tension as the two contrasts meet.

Elijah Adams

Expected to Unexpected Contrast

The expected to unexpected contrast is similar to the rhythm to variation contrast in that both involve repeated elements. Expectation is usually created by repetition with an anticipated sequence of subsequent elements, and the unexpected is an interruption in that anticipated sequence.

The irregular repetition of white extruded lines (right) is contrasted by the single black diagonal wire line. The contrast is enhanced by the shift in material from clay to wire, and in the contrast between black and white.

Aiham Kara Hawa

Shannon Davis

The regular repetition of relief squares (above) is in contrast to the lone negative circle. The contrast of shapes, circle and square, is enhanced by the positive to negative contrast and the dimension to void contrast. The ordered horizontal and vertical repetition of the extruded line (right) contrasts with the transition to a more relaxed and free-flowing organic line that leaves the slab.

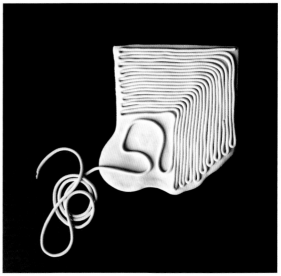

Corrie Cubos

This remarkably restrained mask (right) uses a direct contrast of shape between the elevated circles near the ears and one eye and the single square eye opening. When viewed from the side (below left) the expectation is symmetry in the eye openings; the front view (right) reveals the contrasts and asymmetry.

The regularity of the small grid pattern (bottom row) contrasts dramatically with the large open circles. In a similar way, the straight top edge of the mask contrasts with the curvilinear bottom edge.

Mikey Pena

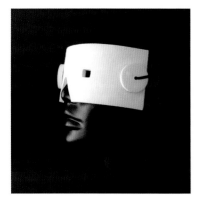

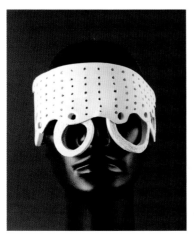

Dannie Wang

Flat to Folded Contrast

This contrast involves the malleable qualities of polymer clay, which allow it to be rolled flat as well as folded like paper or fabric. The contrast in all of the examples compares the flat surface to the unmistakable dimensional surface shown by shade and shadow.

Working with a rolling pin with thickness guides, designers are able to control the depth of the polymer clay slab to create uniform slabs. The most minimal composition consists of only the slab with one folded corner (right). The simplicity of the design is striking, and the contrast

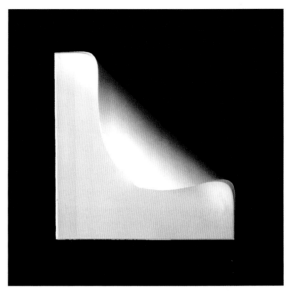

Mira MacDonald

Michiru Morita

is clear as the flat slab corner bends. Other designs employ multiple elements using the ideas of repetition of elements in addition to the transition from flat to folded (below left). The irregularity of the crumpled clay sheets (below right) is appealing and interesting because of the spontaneous, soft, and irregular folds and asymmetric composition.

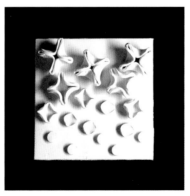

Michiru Morita

Mira MacDonald, Rebecca Miranda

The inspiration for this mask (right) came from the four-inch tile (opposite page, bottom left) by the same designer. In both, the idea of transformation was used to gradually transform the clay disks from flat to folded. In a fabric-like approach (bottom left), the clay is treated as a cloth material revealing a folded smooth side, which covers an eye, and a textured side with an embossed pattern. In yet another mask (bottom right), the clay has soft ripples supported by triangular aluminum pieces and the triangular eye opening is made by gently folding the material away from the face.

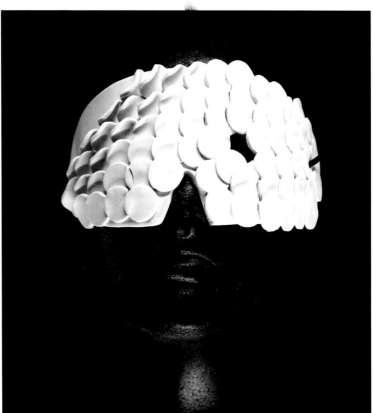

Michiru Morita

Joseph Woods

Martin Pohlmann

Geometric to Organic Contrast

The juxtaposition of the man-made perfection (right) of geometric shapes with unpredictable free-flowing organic shapes is one of the most visually satisfying tile experiments. It is as if the combination fulfills the human craving for perfection in the geometric and for imperfection in free-flowing organic shapes. The tangle of extruded rods appears to be ensnaring the geometric squares.

The direct comparison (below left) of the geometric circles to the curvilinear forms is clear. Circles were cut from a slab (below middle), and the remaining the negative shapes were applied to create irregular organic shapes that contrast with the geometric circles. Tightly rolled ribbons of clay (below right) created geometric circles; then selectively unrolling of the ribbons formed organic shapes.

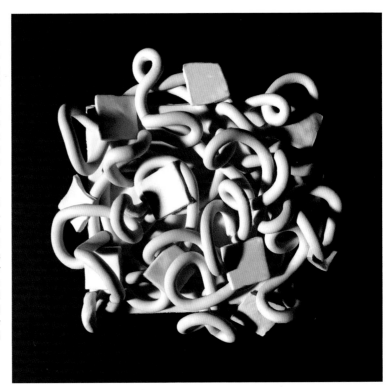

Kelsey Morris

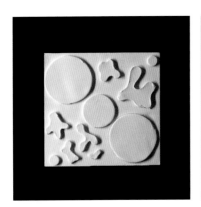

Stephen Moore

Lok Yiu Louise Fung

Mackenzie Schlagenhaft

One eye opening of a mask (below and right) is a geometric circle and the other is an irregular organic shape, establishing contrasting shapes. Additional geometric circle shapes are clustered near the organic eye opening; a single organic shape sits next to the geometric eye. Another mask (bottom row) exhibits a contrast between the circular eye opening and the soft rumpled rectangle of the mask with irregular borders that appear like ripped fabric.

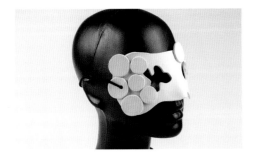

Stephen Moore

Taylor Leitch

Positive to Negative Contrast

Often in the experimental tiles, positive space is perceived as the space occupied by the white clay and negative space as the space occupied by the black background. However, in three-dimensional design, there is a nether space in between positive and negative, which is created by incising elements partway through the slab (right). These elements are white but act as negative because they are deeper and, therefore, on different planes. The perception of space becomes even more ambiguous with overlapping extruded linear shapes in the lower-right quadrant.

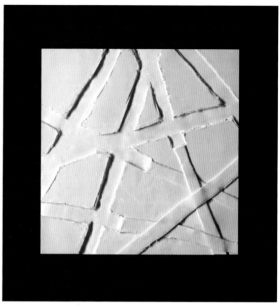

Zackary Miller

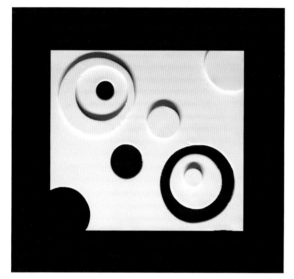

Stephen Moore

The expected white ground of the clay is positive and the cutout voids are negative (above), but the composition is made more interesting by placing circles on top of the slab, which adds another layer of dimension. Another intriguing approach can be seen (right) whereby the positive space is created by the extruded linear shapes that vertically rest on top of the slab. The irregular valleys between the linear shapes become negative space.

Kyle Snider

Brooke Nilsson

Iana Prakheeva

All of these masks have a graphic quality that has been translated into three-dimensional form. The white clay of the masks acts as if it is the positive field; the black cutouts are the negative. The eye openings are all negative spaces, with the single eye opening (below and right) appearing to be a slit between folds of clay.

Noah Selbitschka

Rhythm to Variation Contrast

Rhythm is a sequenced repetition of elements that imply movement. These rhythms can exhibit variation through a change, such as an irregularity or transition. The diagonal dimensional extruded lines (right) move in regular intervals until they are interrupted by intertwined and irregularly arranged lines that create dissonance. The rhythms of the positive and negative circle (below) differ on each row, with variations in sequence as well as in positive and negative space. The coiled circular lines (bottom left) have a subtle change in rhythm as lines

Zackary Miller

overlap as they near the center. Both compositions of incised circles (bottom middle and right) offer a surprise as elements are cropped from the edges and seem to fall off of the square slab.

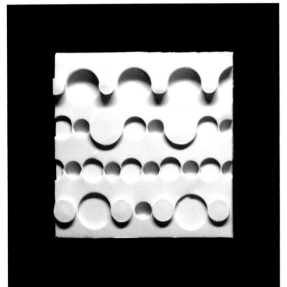

Michiru Morita

Hyeonwoo Alex Cho

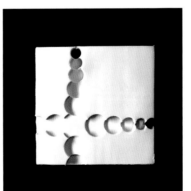

Michiru Morita

Michiru Morita

Regimented diagonal extruded lines create rhythm with variation in the irregular shapes as the lines escape the mask (below and right). It is almost as if the lines are being blown away by wind; there is a sense of fluid movement. In another mask (bottom row), the lines are less regular, with variation occurring in the dissonance of the wire staples holding the two sides of the mask together.

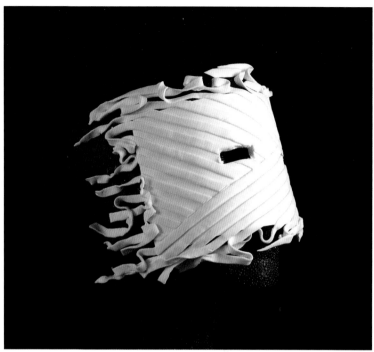

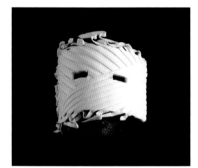

Anissa Rodriguez

Ian Grier

Small to Large Contrast

The small to large contrast is one of scale, which informs the viewer as to the relative largeness or smallness of an object. The most direct method of doing this is to compare like-shaped objects to each other, as does the example with spheres (right). The contrast between the large sphere and the small sphere is enhanced by the dark shadows, which the viewer can compare in addition to the objects themselves. Cropping (below left) is an effective strategy that makes the large circle feel even larger and tension is created as the large circle pushes the small circle toward the edge.

Kelsey Morris

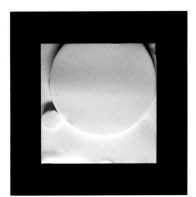

Jackson Dunson

The slightly raised cylinder and spheroid (slightly flattened sphere) composition (bottom right) contrasts the thickness of a thin cylinder with the dimension of a spheroid. Contrasts often overlap and this could also be interpreted as a thick to thin contrast.

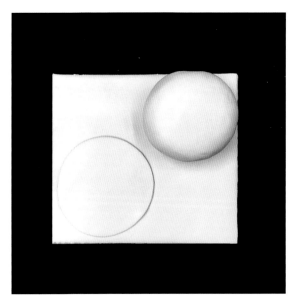

Duncan Demichiel

Rarely do the contrasts occur in isolation, and these masks reveal a scale contrast and an economy to intricacy contrast. The large spheres seem to weigh down the side of the mask (below and right) and cause it to droop beyond the jaw. Similarly, the large triangles seem to grow and cover the eye opening (bottom row), which is in contrast to the small triangles and eye opening visible on the other side. In both masks, the asymmetry is appealing and is enhanced with a single eye opening.

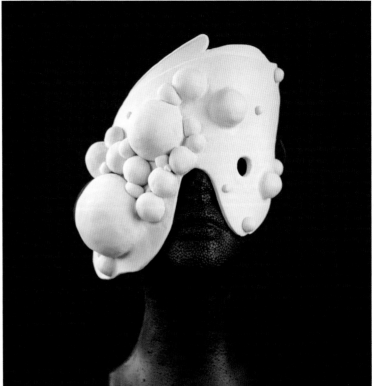

Dan Cantelm

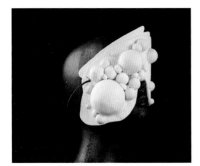

Bria Jackson

Smooth to Rough Contrast

The smooth to rough contrast involves texture and refers to smooth flatness or rough coarseness. Humans are highly conditioned to anticipate sensory experiences in texture, and even when textures are communicated through digital images, they are "felt" with the viewer's mind. The sleek smoothness of the flattened sphere (right) contrasts with the sandpaper-like surface of the square slab. The contrast is not only in the shift in texture but heightened by the interaction between the smooth round shape of the sphere resting on the rough hard-edged square of the background. In the two-circles composition (below right), the shapes are similar and the difference in texture of smooth to rough is obvious. The contrast of elements is subdued because the elements are separated and do not touch each other; contrasts in isolation are not as powerful as when they touch and interact.

Zackary Miller

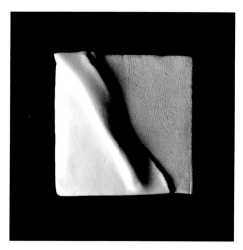

Joseph Woods

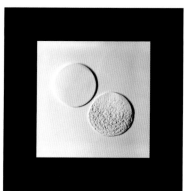

Martin Pohlmann

The straight geometric carved lines (right) contrast with the smooth triangles resting on top. The cracked top layer (far right) seems similar to dried mud with a smooth under layer.

Brady Clem

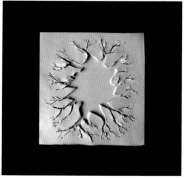

Konrad Losiak

The exaggerated beak-like noses on these masks almost overwhelm the smooth to rough contrast. The scratched pattern around the eye opening (right) meets a jagged crack that is held together with wire staples. The mask below is extended to cover the mouth, yet provides no opening for it, which focuses attention on the single eye opening. The sharp pointed spines starkly contrast to the smooth side.

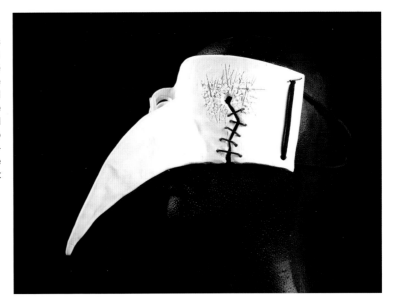

Daniel Salaverri

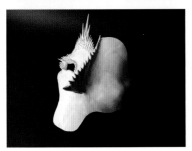

Mira MacDonald

93

Static to Active Contrast

The static to active contrast is similar to the rhythm and variation contrast in that both are dependent on a perceived sense of movement through repetition. Static and active can be portrayed on two separate layers (right). The top layer consists of a flat square in stasis. The bottom layer consists of a repeated diagonal pattern of extruded lines, which imply movement.

The movement of the repeated circles (below) is enhanced by the circle that overlaps the right edge. This is the only full circle in the composition and is the starting

Jeffrey Rozanski

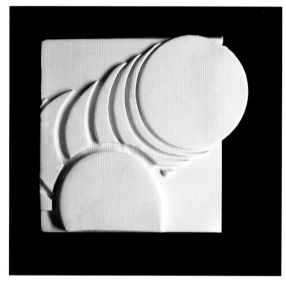

Daniel Cantelm

point for the repeated crescent circles as they move across the slab. The static element, a circle cropped from the bottom edge, interrupts the movement.

The raised square grid pattern (bottom left) can be interpreted as active, and the rows move down the slab until disrupted by a static triangle. The movement suggested by the overlapping incised circles (bottom right) contrasts the immobility of the negative cutout circles that defy movement.

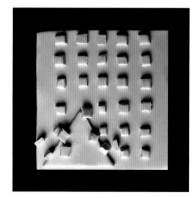

Joseph Woods

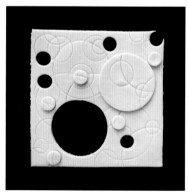

Noman Noman

This mask uses a layered strategy (right and below right): the bottom layer of the mask is a static horizontal/vertical grid pattern of extruded lines. The top layer is active, with repeated incised diagonal lines. Bent wire moves across the mask as if to hold together the static and active layers.

The left eye opening (below) and flat circle that surrounds it forge a focal point from which radiating lines spiral across the mask. This movement, which gently adjusts across the bridge of the nose, is interrupted momentarily by the other eye opening.

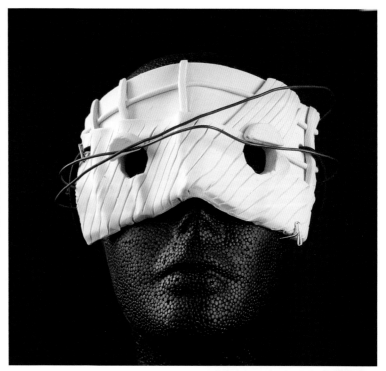

Jingyun Zhou

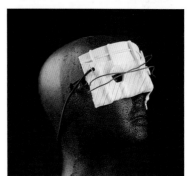

Holly Greaves Brown

Symmetry to Asymmetry Contrast

Symmetry is achieved when elements are arranged equidistantly or mirrored on both sides of an axis. Asymmetry occurs when elements are not arranged equidistantly on both sides of an axis. It is problematic to communicate both symmetry and asymmetry in a single composition, and one of the more inventive solutions to such a limitation involves rotating the composition (right and far right). Seen one way, the composition is symmetrical with the left side mirroring the right side. Rotating the composition results in an asymmetric composition with the four small circles on the left and the two larger circles on the right.

Another strategy uses two separate elements (middle). The split circle represents asymmetry and the whole circle symmetry.

When compared as two halves, the composition of spheres (bottom left) is asymmetric because the left and right sides of the axis do not mirror each other. However, altering the vertical axis to a diagonal on (bottom right) produces symmetry.

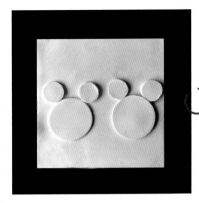

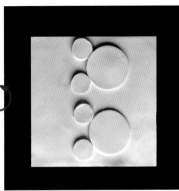

Symmetric Composition
Oskar Flores

Rotated Asymmetric Composition

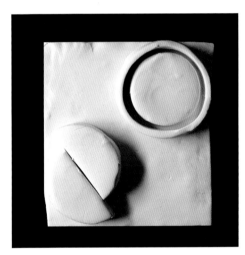

Ian Grier

Asymmetric Composition
Vertical Axis (left)

Symmetric Composition
Diagonal Axis (right)
Teresa Perez

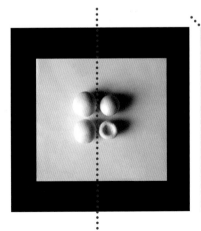

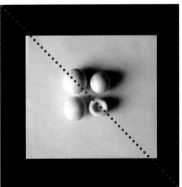

Both of these masks (right and bottom left) are strongly asymmetric. The first thing the viewer notices is that there is only one eye opening per mask. The left side of each mask has an eye opening, and the right side is covered. The designers of these masks, and others in this project, rightly found that asymmetry is far more visually intriguing than symmetry. For comparison purposes, the masks have been digitally manipulated to become symmetric.

Symmetric Mask
Digitally Manipulated Version

Final Asymmetric Mask
Kelly Campbell

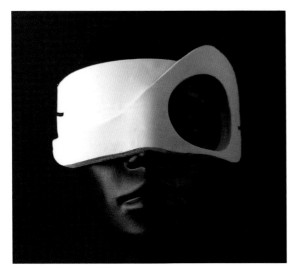

Symmetric Mask
Digitally Manipulated Version

Final Asymmetric Mask
Caio Arias Nogueira

Tension to Relaxation Contrast

Tension is an indication of stress and is created through the interaction of elements. Relaxation is the release of tension to a more neutral state. One strategy is to portray tension as chaotic energy, which can be seen in the tangles of extruded lines (right). Release occurs as the lines unwind, relax, and comfortably encircle the tangle. Another strategy is to portray the tangle as the relaxed state (below left) and tension as the regular and regimented lines in the slab. A third strategy (below right) involves a texture of deep crowded holes on the lower left corner ebbing to a texture of comfortable sparseness and shallowness toward the upper right corner.

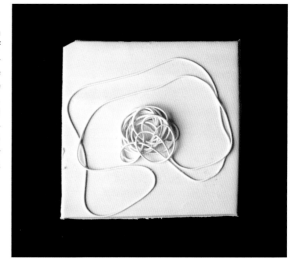

Corrie Cubos

Mikey Pena

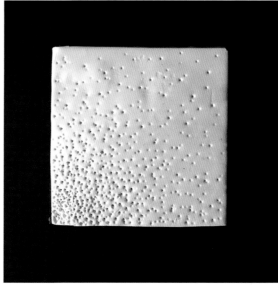

Hyeonwoo Alex Cho

In both of these masks, tension is portrayed with tightly controlled, straight, and regimented lines that transform into much more relaxed, irregular curvilinear lines. In the bottom example, the extruded lines seem to relax to the point of dripping down the face.

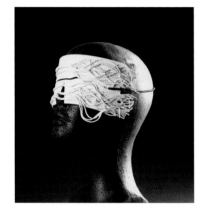

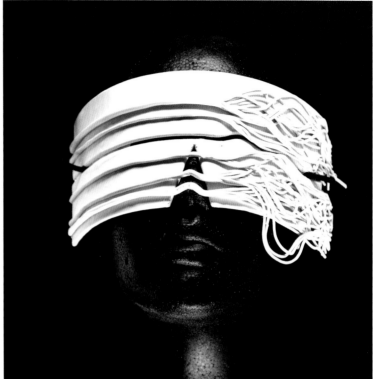

Michiru Morita

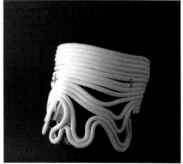

Rebecca Miranda

Penguin
Yuri Priamo-Canales

Giraffe
Renata Molnar

Camera
Mikey Pena

Rooster
Andrea Menéndez

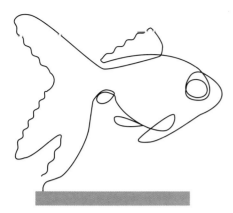

Goldfish
Roy Chasteen

Chapter 3. The Three-Dimensional Line, Wire Icons

The inspiration for this project comes from the wonderfully minimal continuous-line drawings, which are often used in logo design. These drawings are brilliantly simple, and the eye follows each line from the beginning, around the object, over the loops, to the end. They're visually satisfying expressions of the bare bones of what information is needed for communication.

Simplifying an animal, person, or an object to a single line drawing is an intriguing challenge. The challenges and complexity are amplified when the line is three-dimensional wire and exists in space. Intricate details are quickly eliminated because of the difficulty in shaping wire and because the focus is on identifying shapes. The necessity of the wire compositions to be freestanding encourages a sense of balance that is not always present or necessary in two-dimensional drawings.

Sculpting with wire is a complex activity that involves the merging of the representational and the stylized. This project uses a focused methodology to create an icon in two and three dimensions with a single continuous line. The line becomes alive, fluidly describing the object in silhouette as well as in selected interior features, details, and surfaces. The methodology guides the student through a design process with optimal opportunities for both creativity and success.

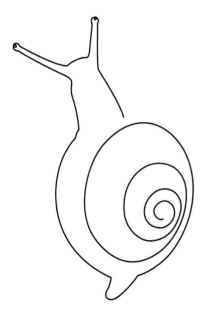

Snail
Thomas Pregiato

Snail
Teresa Perez

Project Process Overview

An analysis of continuous-line drawings, particularly line logos, can assist in understanding the process of simplification and abstraction. Continuous-line logos are often minimal line drawings that have pleasing proportions and refined arcs and curves. This is because the designer has succeeded in reducing the iconicity of the object to the minimum with only selected interior-or-surface clues while retaining the recognizability of the object or creature.

Understanding how other artists and designers work with wire can provide vital information regarding craft techniques and composition. It is through analysis of research and discussion of composition that strategies can be established for the creation of focal points, the development of continuous-line eye flow, the closure and capturing of space, and determining the beginning and termination of wire lines.

Continuous-Line Drawing Research

Bee

Butterfly

Snail

Rooster
Audrey Oleshko, designer

Wire Sculpture Research

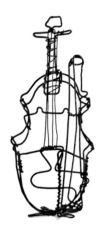

Cello

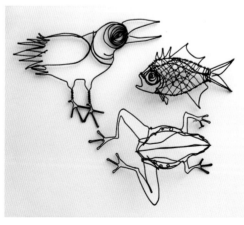

F is for Frog, Fish, Fowl
Thomas Hill, sculptor

Birds and Dog

Found visual material is used as a tool by tracing over the photograph or drawing. This permits experimentation on how a continuous line can best describe the subject. Shown below (top row) are a series of drawings that experiment with describing the subject with a single line. The line origin and ending are important because the wire will need to start in a wood base and terminate in a manner that is satisfying with the visual composition. Multiple explorations of this process result in a continuous-line drawing suitable for wirework.

Next, the hand-drawn graphic drawing is scanned and used as a computer-generated drawing template. The computer drawing is further stylized with vector-drawing tools to create a crisp line icon. Shown (middle row) are final computer drawings of the subject based on the selected hand-drawn graphic drawings. In the final phase of the project (bottom row), the computer drawing is used as a template to create a three-dimensional wire sculpture.

Continuous-Line Drawing

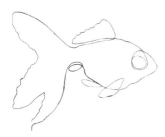  

Computer-Graphic Drawing

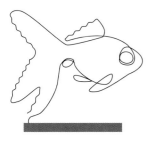  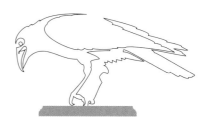

Wire Sculpture

Before commencing work on a line icon and in order to understand the qualities of wire and how to work with wire, an object is chosen and a wire sculpture of the object is made. A natural process of abstraction occurs as portions are necessarily and selectively left out of the outline, creating closure and capturing space. The objective is not to recreate the object with wire but to visually describe the essence of the three-dimensional form with wire lines.

Wire Craft Exploration

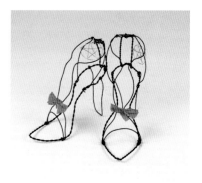

Jasmine Jang

Student Work, Kim Litch, Instructor

Student Work, Kim Litch, Instructor

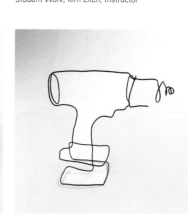

Mikey Pena

Student Work, Kim Litch, Instructor

Student Work, Kim Litch, Instructor

Butterfly

As with a number of line icons, the initial butterfly drawings focused on the silhouette. While the silhouette is
descriptive, it leaves much to be desired in describing
the butterfly. The addition of symmetrical wing segments, or interior loops, adds considerably to the visual
description. The wire sculpture includes wings that are
offset by a zigzag wire line that implies the body shape
and terminates in an arc that launches the butterfly
from the base.

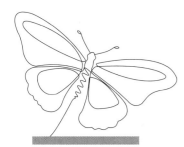

Computer Vector Drawing

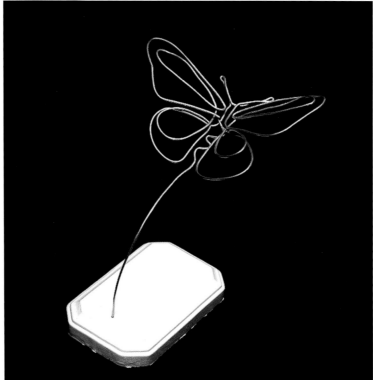

Butterfly Wire Sculpture
Philip Clark
Jeff Bleitz, Instructor

Line Drawings from Research

Elephant

During the initial drawing phase of the project, the starting point of the line shifted from the rear leg to the front leg to better describe the silhouette. The loops in the computer drawing and wire model are an effective device to describe the wrinkles in the trunk, the knees, and the small wisp of a tail. These loops not only define the surface but also give the viewer a visual pause as the eye follows the line; they also unify the drawing and sculpture through repetition.

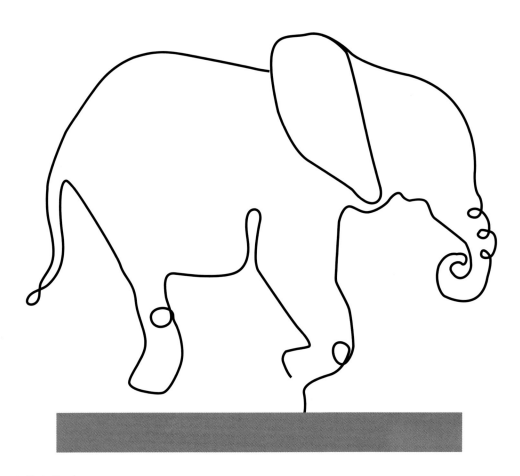

Computer Vector Drawing

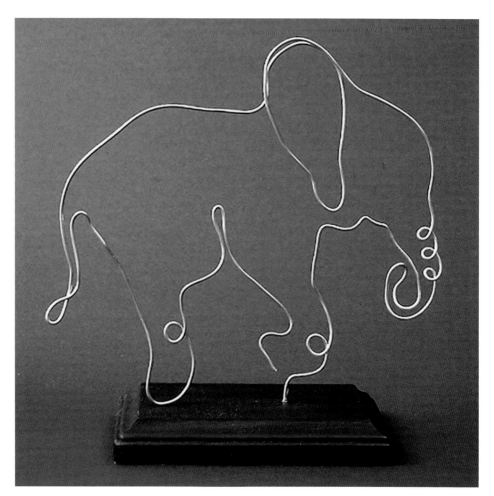

Elephant Wire Sculpture
Marcos Roman

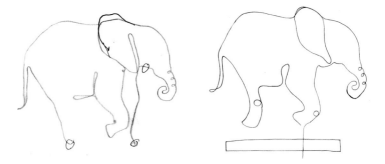

Line Drawings from Research

Flamingo

The elegant form of the flamingo is apparent in both the vector-line drawing and the wire sculpture. Three loops, including the eye, wing, and knee, create balance and a harmonious contrast to the straight leg line. The single leg extends up from the base as if it is standing in water, with the unseen leg tucked underneath the body.

Computer Vector Drawing

Flamingo Wire Sculpture
Laura Temple

Goldfish

The first drawings of the goldfish were simple silhouettes. As work progressed, the goldfish became more detailed and included the rhythm and repetition of the ruffled fin edges and a number of loops. The repeated loops of the eye become a point of focus and offer a moment of visual rest. Loops in the fins show the wire moving as fluidly as the fish does in water.

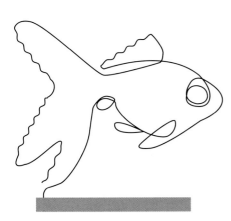

Computer Vector Drawing

Goldfish Wire Sculpture
Roy Chasteen

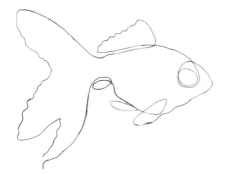

Line Drawing from Research

Giraffe

The initial drawings of the giraffe were highly complex, with the line describing the spots in negative space in a mazelike fashion. As the drawings progressed, the spots were simplified as were the details in the legs and hooves. This process of reduction and abstraction continued, with the number and complexity of spots reduced to a minimum, as the model was created in wire.

Computer Vector Drawing

Giraffe Wire Sculpture
Renata Molnar
Jeff Bleitz, Instructor

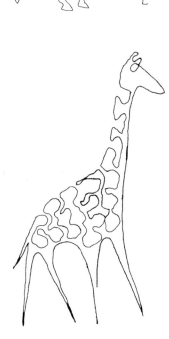

Line Drawings from Research

Gorilla

The pose of the gorilla changed from static to active during the design process. Initially, the gorilla was standing at rest. By the conclusion of the vector drawing, the base had become a platform, with the gorilla stepping up and onto it. The face of the gorilla is expressive, with a visual loop for the eye. One of the arms is partially hidden, which adds visual interest. Both the line beginning and ending are punctuated with a loop.

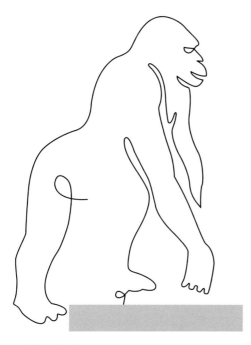

Computer Vector Drawing

Gorilla Wire Sculpture
Amanda Clark

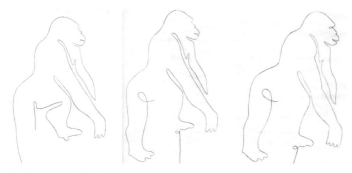

Line Drawings from Research

Hammerhead Shark

The dynamic pose of the hammerhead shark shows it leaping from the stand. The wire captures the highlights on the body and the repetition in the edges of the hammerhead and gills. The small teeth in the mouth of the initial drawings (bottom row) were eliminated due to the scale of the model. The fluid curves of the fins invite the eye to follow the contour of the shark.

Hammerhead Wire Sculpture
Mike Munger

Computer Vector Drawing

Line Drawings from Research

Hedgehog and Baby

The rhythm and repetition of soft spinelike forms guide the viewer's eye along the backs of the mama and baby hedgehogs. Similar loops form the legs and nose, and the line terminates in a spiral that becomes the eye. Each creature is designed with the economy of a single line.

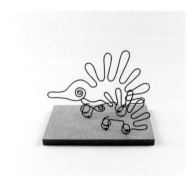

Hedgehog Wire Sculpture
Martin Pohlmann

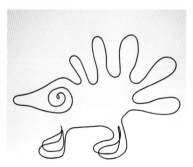

Rough Prototype
The form of the hedgehog developed from a quick rough model of imprecise form. With each subsequent model the ideas of the spiral and repetition of spines were developed and refined.

Iguana

The iguana is one of the more complex line icons and the designer chose a green, lightweight, floral wire for construction. The thin wire enabled the designer to capture the details of the spines and the cheek circles on the jowl. The rhythm of the spines extends along the back and under the throat. The repetition of circles begins at the eye and appears in the nose, cheek, elbow, and toes.

Computer Vector Drawing

Iguana Wire Sculpture
Melike Turgut

Line Drawings from Research

Monkey

The inspiration for the monkey's pose came from a necklace of a figure hanging from a chain. A similar pose was used and required that the wire start from the base as the pole from which the monkey would hang. The minimal silhouette is beautifully interrupted by a loop that defines the monkey's shoulder. The pose is delightful, and the figure has a sense of swinging motion.

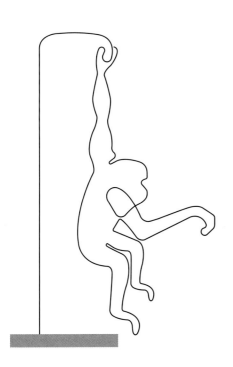

Computer Vector Drawing

Monkey Wire Sculpture
Michael Johnston

Penguin

The active toddling pose of the penguin is captivating as it appears to be stepping off of the base. The wire line transition from flipper to flipper suggests the change in color from dark flippers to white chest and terminates in a spiral on the chest. This spiral is reflected in the loop that forms the eye.

Computer Vector Drawing

Penguin Wire Sculpture
Yuri Priamo-Canales

Ram

The ram head began as a full sheep figure (bottom right)
and quickly evolved to concentrate only on the head.
The focal point is the spiral horn, which commences as
a loop for the eye and repeats in diminishing size as it
tapers to the end of the horn. These loops repeat in the
nose, neck, and as the wire travels down to the base.

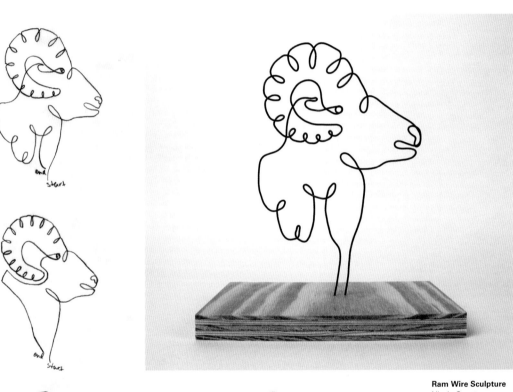

Ram Wire Sculpture
Nicole Constance

Line Drawings from Research

Rooster

The irregular and complex line work of the rooster is delightful and captures the essence of the bird. Instead of trying to stylize the tail feathers into a regimented pattern, they are casual and irregular, with loops appearing at each moment of change in direction. The same system is used for the wing, comb, and wattle, which contribute to the sense of compositional cohesiveness. The wing that occupies negative space adds visual interest to the project.

Computer Vector Drawing

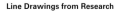

Rooster Wire Sculpture
Andrea Menéndez

Line Drawings from Research

Fishes

The hanging fish is a very minimalist wire icon. The wire barely describes a series of three generic fish, yet the use of hooks and the hanging of the three individual fish with fishing line provide sufficient visual clues for viewer understanding. The composition of three differently sized fish is visually satisfying, and the eye follows the continuous line in each figure.

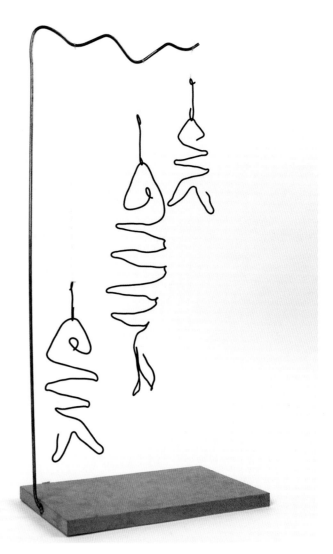

Fish Wire Sculpture
Noah Jennings

Snail 1

The spiral shape of the snail shell was the inspiration for this wire model. The wire whorls capture space by spiraling up from the body. The tight curves contrast the triangular upper tentacles and the lower tentacles, which move horizontally away from the spiral shell.

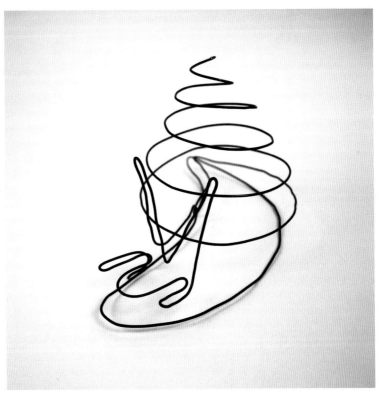

Snail 1 Wire Sculpture
Teresa Perez

Snail 2

The snail is one of the most elegant wire icons. The silhouette is immediately recognizable, and the line spirals to form the shell. The eye cannot help but follow the line to the end. Rather than use a stand, the designer envisioned a snail clinging to a tree branch and found a piece of weathered wood for that purpose.

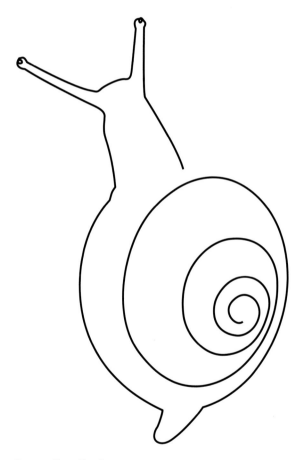

Computer Vector Drawing

Line Drawings from Research

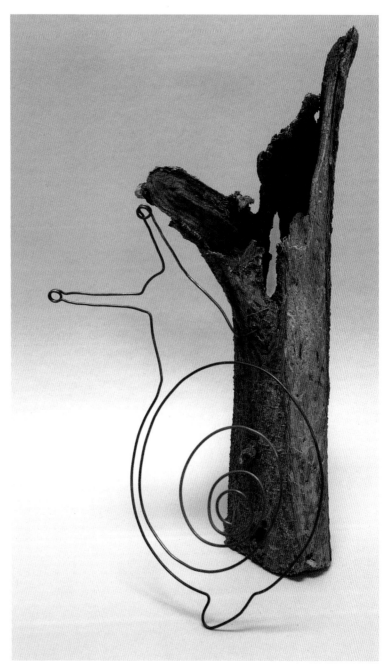

Snail 2 Wire Sculpture
Thomas Pregiato

Lemon
C. Ayelen Rosales

Cauliflower
Yuri Priamo-Canales

Radicchio
Chris Haslup

Watermelon
Elsa Chaves
Jeff Bleitz, Instructor

Chapter 4. Packaging and Abstraction, Paper Food

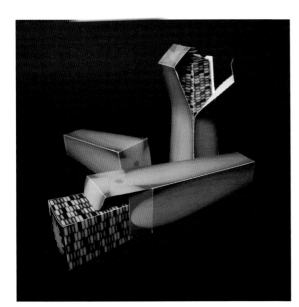

Corn
Rob Kautz

Most people think of natural foods in terms of simple shapes and solid colors, such as a curved banana with yellow skin and pale flesh or a spherical red tomato with yellowish seeds inside. Closer examination, however, reveals subtle changes and details in the color, textures, and patterns of the surface foods. Pears, for example, transform as they ripen, from green to blush to yellow, and a closer look reveals a delicate speckled pattern in the skin that also changes color and is rarely noticed.

Paper Food examines and reveals these colors and patterns through graphic textures and simplified shapes, and its packages are designed to be abstract three-dimensional representations of food products. These packages join the graphic design of texture and color based on a food item with the three-dimensional construction of a package fold pattern. Often, the packages are conceptual representations that show the method of peeling or slicing the food. Corn husks with perforated edges are peeled down, and tomatoes are sliced cross sections stacked together. The project intent is to experience the process of close observation and through design reinterpret a food product as a three-dimensional package.

Tomato
Dane Overton

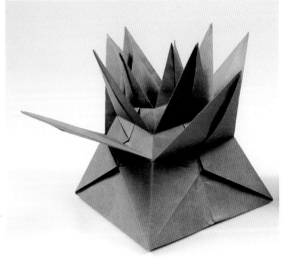

Artichoke
Sarah Al-Wassia

Project Process Overview

The project began with the selection of a food product. When possible, it was brought into class to be studied and photographed. If the food was not available, photographs were collected to carefully examine the color, shape, and texture. Based on this visual research, the student graphically abstracted the color and texture of the food, resulting in a simplified graphic color and texture that was applied to the paperboard package.

Next, a geometric carton was designed for the food. Since the carton is constructed with paperboard, the shape consists of straight lines and angles that can be scored and folded into a closed carton. The goal was a simplified geometric shape rather than an attempt at a re-creation of the shape with a complex fold pattern. A tapered carton was designed for the pear because it related to the sloped shape of the fruit. In this example, the pear carton has an outer shell that can be "peeled" away by lifting it up, revealing two inner halves of the fruit and the seeds. The graphics and fold pattern are printed on card stock, with which the paper food carton is constructed.

Visual Research

  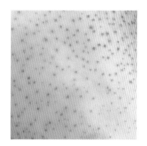

Color and Pattern

  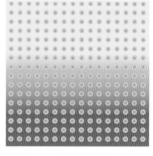

Green Dot Pattern   Gradient Color   Dot Pattern and Gradient Color

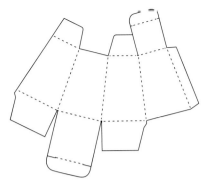

Carton and Fold Pattern

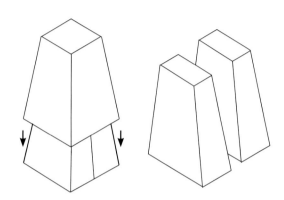

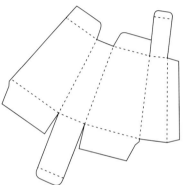

Exterior (top) and Interior (bottom) Carton Fold Pattern

Isometric Drawing

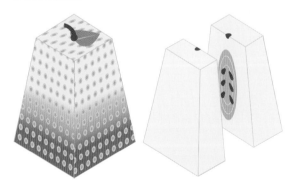

Pear Paper Food Package

Amanda Clark

There is a thriving community of paper food artists and designers that can be found online. Some create paper food as a delightful hobby while others create for print and online media. What makes these inventions interesting is that they are two- and three-dimensional abstraction and paper portrayals of familiar foods. This research process serves as inspiration for both the two- and three-dimensional abstraction as well as the highest level of paper-crafting skills.

Paper Taco
Maria Laura Benavente Sovieri, mililitros.com

Paper Craft Research

Paper Pineapple

Paper Strawberry

Paper Hamburger

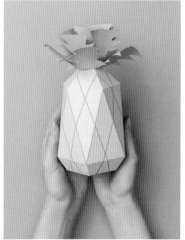

Paper Pineapple

Paper Ice Cream Cones

Paper Pear

Paper Watermellon

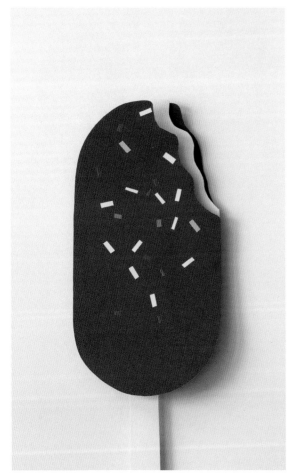

Paper Ice Cream Bar

Paper Orange and Orange Juice

Paper Food Models and Drawings

Artichoke and Avocado

This designer was fascinated with the traditional craft of origami and researched origami fold patterns. A lightweight origami paper was used to shape an artichoke. Multiple versions of the artichoke were created, with each version slightly smaller than the previous one so they could be nested. A pyramid cap completes the package.

The package of the avocado is a simple dark green tapered rectangle, accented by a self-adhesive supermarket sticker. The two halves are held together by a friction fit pit. When pulled apart, the avocado reveals the sliced flesh of the avocado.

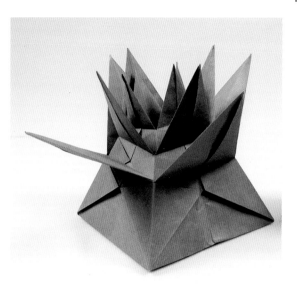

Sarah Al-Wassia

Christopher Roeleveld

Banana

The banana package is a study in simplicity. The yellow exterior packaging is hinged at the top and cut at an angle so as to peel open. The irregular brown spots reference the change in color that occurs during ripening. A stacked series of banana-patterned interior segments, with banana cross-section graphics, complete the product inside the package.

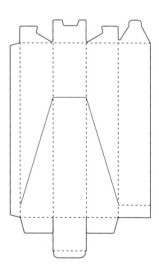

Isometric Drawing

Fold Pattern

Rob Kautz

Cabbage

The cabbage is a box within a box that peels apart, or unfolds. The hinged four-sided segments come together to overlap and form a cube. The irregularity of the top panel segments echoes the leaves of a cabbage, and the organic pattern of shadowed veins complete the Paper Food box.

Chris Haslup

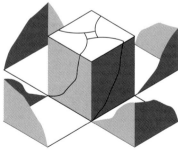

Isometric Drawings

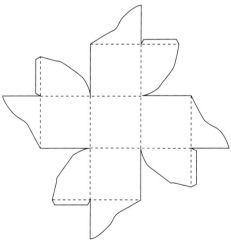

Fold Pattern

Corn

Indian corn, with its interesting and irregular changes in color was chosen as the concept for this package. The exterior consists of a series green and yellow/green ellipses that represent the husk, with perforated edges that permit the husk to be peeled away from the cob, revealing the brightly colored Indian corn cob.

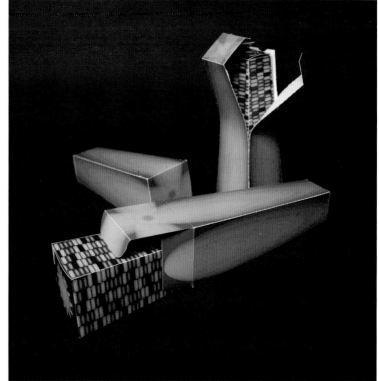

Rob Kautz

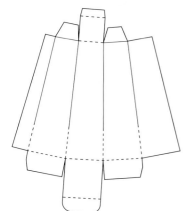

Fold Pattern

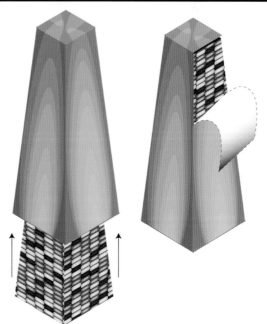

Isometric Drawings

Carrots

Carrots are often thought of in bunches; therefore, three paperboard carrots are fastened together with a produce rubber band. The box is made employing a long tapered fold pattern on bright orange paper. The top closure is fastened with a decorative metal paper clip.

Fortune Cookie

The fortune cookie package is a geometric interpretation of the traditional form. Smooth brown cardboard was used to simulate the color, and a perforated crease allows the package to be broken open to reveal the fortune.

Heidi Dyer

Elsa Chaves
Jeff Bleitz, Instructor

Isometric Drawing

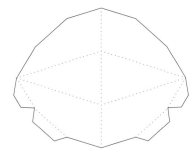

Fold Pattern

Grapefruit

Below are two different interpretations of a grapefruit. The top example is a simple gift package with semi-circular flaps, which allude to the spherical form of the fruit. When the package is opened, an interior cube printed with geometric pink grapefruit cross sections is revealed. The exterior of the bottom box features a delicate stippled pattern of a grapefruit's rind. The fine dot pattern is random and asymmetric, with just a slight difference in tone separating the pattern color from the background color. The interior package represents the two halves of a cut grapefruit.

Isometric Drawing

Felicia Koloc

Pattern Drawing

Ben Rupp

Hamburger

The hamburger differs from the other Paper Food projects in that it is made of multiple components and is a man-made food. The exterior box of the hamburger package mimics the familiar fast food package. Once opened, a series of hexagonal packages represent the hamburger, the layers serving the bun, the pickles and ketchup, a thin layer of mayonnaise, and the hamburger patty. A graphic pattern of sesame seeds decorates the bun top.

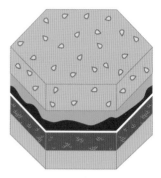

Isometric Drawing

John Huffman

Orange

The orange package employs a method of opening that involves peeling along perforations in the paper. Once opened, two graphic cross-section halves of the fruit are revealed. The pattern for the exterior is a vibrant combination of green-on-yellow and yellow-on-green dots placed on top of a solid orange background. A graphic leaf extends from the top to the side as an accent.

Peach

The peach is strongly graphic both outside and inside. The outer package, or skin, has a double dot pattern on a surface that is a gradient of orange to red, which is similar to the blush of a peach. Stylized leaves on the top of the package break up the regimented pattern. The interior halves of the peach package feature crevices that house a paperboard pit. The graphics on the halves echo the change of color and form of the peach flesh that occur after the pit is removed.

Felicia Koloc

Amanda Clark

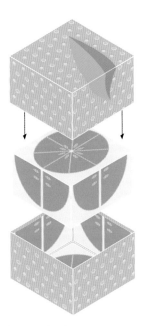

Isometric Drawing

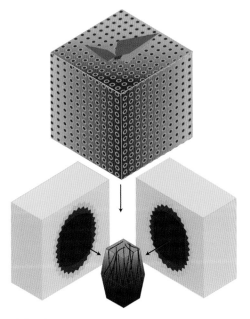

Isometric Drawing

Pear

The delicateness of the surface of the pear is evident in the patterns made for the package. The designer created two different organic patterns (below, Loop Pattern and Brush Pattern), which rest on top of a solid yellow-green surface. A radial gradient creates a blush that spans two sides of the box, on which a produce sticker is placed. Instead of a folding box or a slipcase, the box hinge opens the package, unveiling a delicately detailed cross section of the fruit.

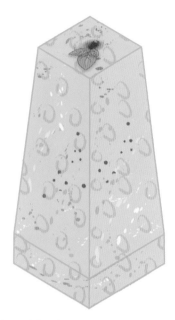

Isometric Drawing

Marcos Roman

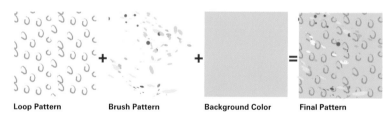

| Loop Pattern | Brush Pattern | Background Color | Final Pattern |

Patterns

Two different patterns are overlaid on top of the solid green background to create the final surface.

Scallions

The very thin and elongated scallion was a challenge to recreate in a paper package. The designer chose to increase the scale of the scallion in a prism package and to make a number of packages bound as a bunch. Delicate gradient color and root details at the carton end accent the package and make it unmistakably a scallion.

Tomato

The concept for the tomato package was to drastically reduce both the scale and graphics to the bare minimum. The exterior package is a bright red solid slipcase accented with a green star stem-end. The interior is a single tomato cross-section slice, identified by highly abstracted yet familiar graphics.

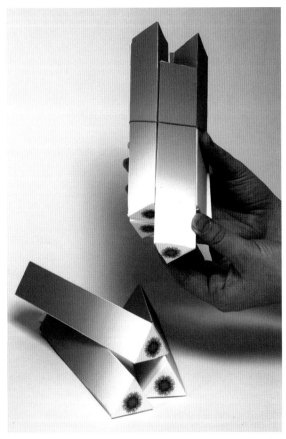

Lenna Dahlquist

Dane Overton
Jeff Bletiz, Instructor

Cross-Section Drawing

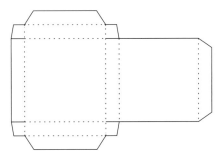

Fold Pattern

Watermelon 1

This watermelon was visualized as a cylindrical container. Multiple layers of green tissue paper were glued onto paperboard to create the striped exterior rind pattern. When the cap is pulled off, there are four watermelon wedges accented by white rind, bright red flesh, and seeds.

Watermelon 2

This watermelon was abstracted into the shape of a rectangle. Bold, highly graphic zigzag stripes mimic the rind pattern, which is interrupted by a stem-end. The interior graphics and shapes follow the visual theme: the removable wedges are strikingly abstract.

Elsa Chaves
Jeff Bleitz, Instructor

Heather Clark

Isometric Drawings

Watermelon 3

The stripes of the watermelon rind are created with an inventive multiple-dot pattern. This dot pattern softens the white edges of the rind and makes them feel organic. The exterior rind is a slipcase that wraps around the interior of four hinged slices. The visual theme of the dot pattern reappears in the cross section of the rind, which is made of white dots.

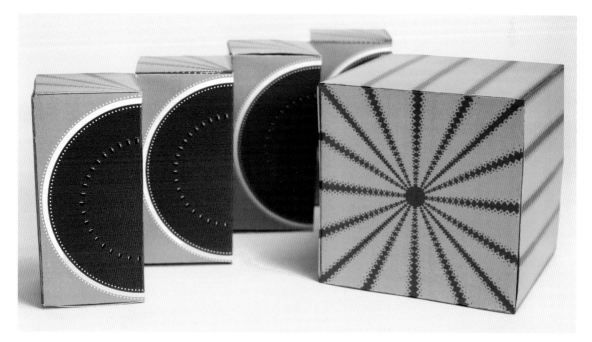

Phillip Clark
Jeff Bleitz, Instructor

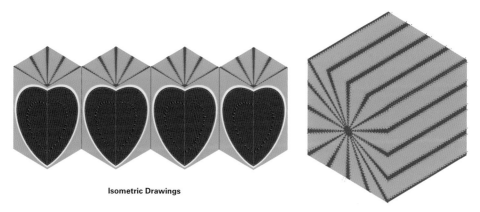

Isometric Drawings

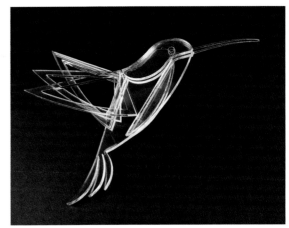

Hummingbird
Ikkamatti Hauru

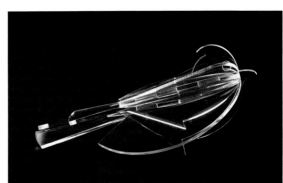

Kinglet
Martin Pholmann

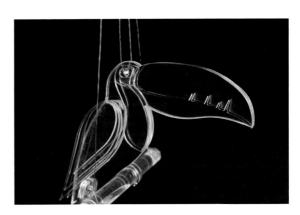

Toucan
Stephen Moore

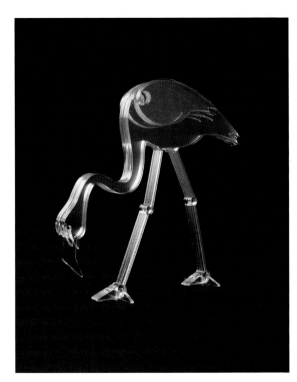

Flamingo
Sophia Holland

Chapter 5. Multiplane Acrylic Birds

One of the most distinctive features of some birds is vibrant coloring. The thought of a cardinal, flamingo, or parrot immediately evokes in the mind bright red, pink, and green. Because of this, the most challenging aspect of this project was to create a bird without color, in clear acrylic. Some birds, such as flamingos, have a truly distinctive shape and features, including a long sinuous neck and very elongated legs. They are relatively easy to identify by shape, but many others are far more difficult to determine by silhouette.

The shape of a bird must be carefully examined, and the many nuances of physical details in the proportions of beaks, eyes, bodies, and wings must be recognized. Body and wing shapes were simplified and abstracted into a series of clear planes that became the core of the model. Both bold and subtle differences in color were communicated through changes in the shape of over-lapping or offset planes.

Clear sheet acrylic plastic is a beautiful yet unforgiving material. It was chosen because of its translucent and reflective qualities; light travels to the edges to create highlights and reveal the form. This delicate lightness is in keeping with the sleek and aerodynamic shapes of birds.

Cockatoo
Teresa Perez

143

Project Process Overview

An understanding of the key features and basic proportions of a particular bird through visual research enables the drawing to closely resemble that bird. Line drawings show the individual shapes; this method was preferred in this project because line drawings reveal how shapes can become individual overlapping planes in clear acrylic. Drawings were done with vector computer software since the bird would be laser cut from a vector file.

Next, the line drawing's individual shapes were separated and extruded with computer software. The extruded pieces were aligned and the opacity was reduced to show how the bird would look as a transparent three-dimensional object. Planes could easily be added, deleted, or adjusted in this drawing.

Line Drawings

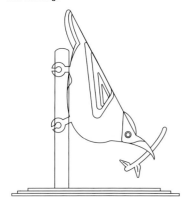

Ellie Winslow

Ayse Dilan Taylan

Teresa Perez

Extruded Drawings

The final test before laser cutting was to make a three-dimensional foam model. The paper skins were stripped from both sides of a foam-core board, leaving only the foam center, which was then trimmed, sanded, and assembled. The foam center is much easier to cut without the paper skin. This prototype model allowed for final refinement and adjustment of all of the model pieces.

The last phase of the project was to use the drawing to create a laser-cutting pattern. All pieces were separated and the sheet acrylic was measured with a caliper to ensure that interlocking pieces would fit together cleanly. Sheet acrylic is cut with the laser-cutting machine, and the heat of the laser cleanly polishes the edges for a finished result.

Foam Prototype Models

Laser-Cut Acrylic Models

Shape Language

Simplification of the bird into a series of clear acrylic planes includes geometrically interpreting the bird form and creating a shape language. A shape language is the fluid use of a repeated shape or portions of a shape that, when used together, create a figure. In this project, the shape language was based on geometric shapes, such as circle, triangle, or square. The use of a shape language enables the parts of a drawing to relate to each other and can often help result in a cohesive composition.

The geometric elements used in a shape language do not need be a strict interpretation conforming to a single shape. The repeated use of a part of the element, such as a corner arc or radius, is often enough to echo the theme. Additionally, the use of tangent shapes that touch or flow into one another is a highly effective technique that unifies the shape language by enabling the viewer's eye to move throughout the drawing.

Arcs and Lines
The upside-down hanging Eurasian nuthatch is composed of a series of shapes, each having an arc that transitions to a straight line. The arcs are tangent to the lines and are present in the white breast of the bird as negative shapes. Triangles are repeated in the negative space between the legs as well as in the body shapes and beak.

Eurasian Nuthatch, Josh Brill, illustrator

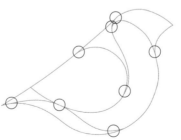

Tangents
The bullfinch is more subtle in that the component shapes appear similar but only vaguely so. Each shape has both an arc and a taper to a point. Although the individual shapes are different, each shape is tangent to another as they appear to flow from one into another. In the diagram, the tangent points are identified with red circles.

Bullfinch, Ivan Bobrov, illustrator

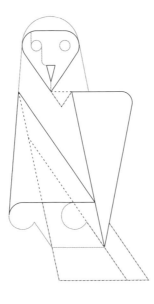

Triangles

The rhythm and repetition of the triangles in the body make this composition cohesive. Although the shape of the triangle varies, the way in which they are tangent to other shapes unifies the composition. The beak triangle is emphasized by color as it's the only pinkish element and rests at the center of the face. The eye circles are echoed in the face triangle with rounded corners and the two circles at the feet.

Barn Owl, Josh Brill, illustrator

Teardrops

The dodo, now extinct, is composed of a teardrop shape at the tip of the beak and two similar shapes nested in the body. The teardrop is related to the circle, which forms the eye. The arcs and curves of the teardrop contrast the rectangular feet and color change to a musty green.

Dodo, Josh Brill, illustrator

Acrylic Bird Models and Drawings

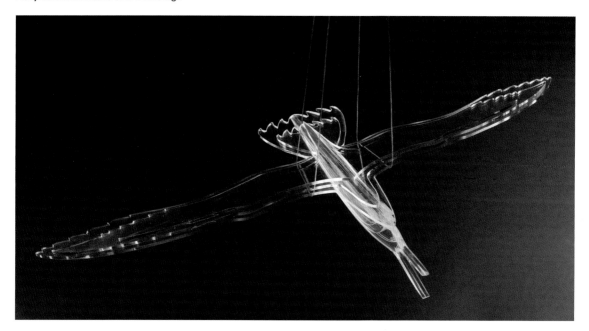

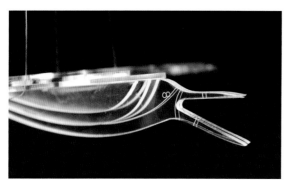
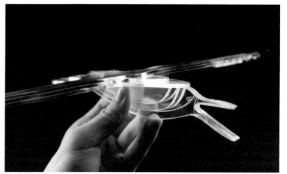

John Gnieski

Hanging Bird in Flight

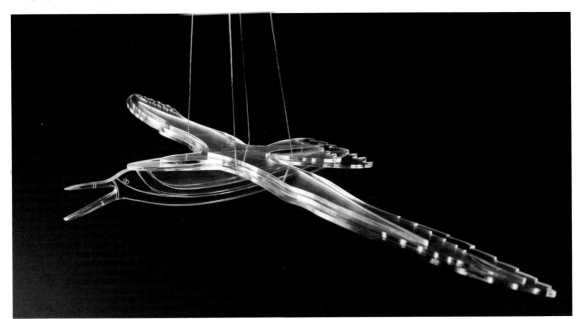

From the earliest concept sketches, this bird was designed to have the illusion of flight by hanging. The long wingspan utilizes multiple layers of clear acrylic, as does the body. Small details of an eye and lines are etched or scored partway into the acrylic. Due to the weight and size of the model, an additional monofilament line was used to balance the hanging gull.

The Illusion of Movement

Both of these hummingbirds use repetition to create the illusion of rapid wing movement. Initial draw-ings portrayed the wings as repeated solid shapes but evolved to become outlines in order to emphasize the delicacy of the wings and the qual-ity of vibration. As outlined shapes the wings increase in complexity because the overlapping outlines create additional negative spaces.

Ian Grier

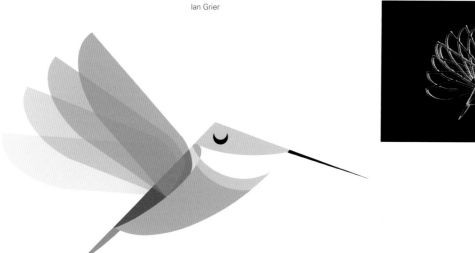

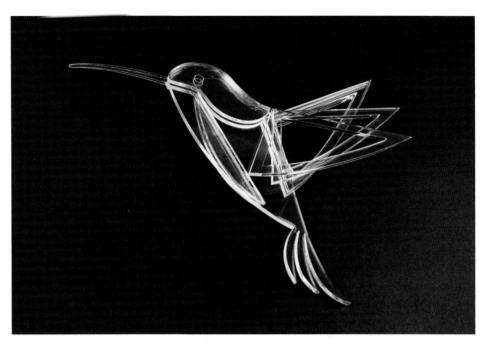

Ikkamatti Hauru

Avery Lashbrook

The positions of the ostrich feet and legs suggests that it is going to step off of the acrylic base, with the forward leg balancing on a small tapered toe. The pose is dynamic and imbues the acrylic model with a sense of life and movement. The bird is drawn and modeled with only straight lines, giving the figure harsh angles. Some of these angles combine to define the head and long neck; others layer to act as the planes of the wings and tail feathers.

Each wing of the hummingbird is composed of multiple overlapping shapes, which produces a sense of rapid rhythmical movement. The model is hung from monofilament lines, and the body position mimics that of a hummingbird getting ready to sip nectar from a flower.

Amber Johnson

Wading Birds

Wading birds are standing birds with reedy thin legs. As a consequence, consideration must be given to the strength of the material and the best method with which to balance the model. Each of these three different wading birds uses a different structure to enable the model to stand. The designer of the heron (right) initially used thin acrylic legs but later employed wrapped wire for the legs and feet. The wire not only provides strong support but also contrasts in color and texture with the body. For additional contrast, the designer sanded the lower part of the body to create the appearance of white on a clear acrylic model. The base is faux rock.

Nikki Alese

154

Jeffrey Rozanski

The wading bird (top row) uses an acrylic base as a means to anchor the bird. This base provides support, and the small tufts of marsh grass offers an environment that prevents the base from appearing as an afterthought.

The appeal of the food-searching pose of the flamingo (above and right) comes from the multiple curves in the neck that contrast with straight lines of the legs. The flamingo legs were strengthened by sandwiching three layers of acrylic together, providing the stability necessary for the bird to comfortably stand, and is reinforced with a small crosspiece in each foot.

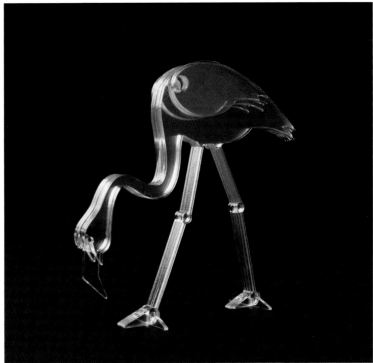

Sophia Holland

Birds on Perches or Stands

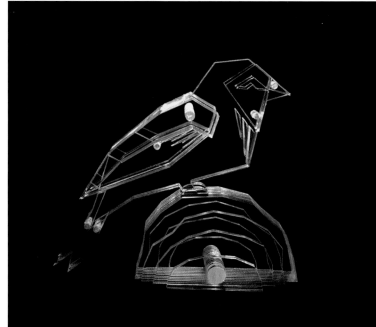

Duncan Demichiel

Jingyun Zhou

Birds designed to be fixed to a base or object need to have care given to the selection and development of the pose in relationship to the perch or stand. This is done to avoid feeling like the base was an afterthought. The birds are static abstractions, and the positions of the body and the way the legs join the stand are important in communicating the form. The small finch (opposite page, top row) is composed entirely of straight lines and is perched on an abstracted rock also made of straight lines around an arc. Because of the shared straight-line construction, the bird and the rock seem to belong together. The cardinal (opposite page, bottom row) benefits from a diagonal branch and the diagonal leg positions, which makes the bird appear to be moving. The angles also contrast with the rounded shapes of the bird. Multiple layers of clear acrylic were used to give the bird volume, and a clear dowel fixed the wings to the body. The base is an ellipse, which echoes similar shapes of the body.

The highly stylized gull (below) almost looks like a hood ornament of a vintage car. Only geometric shapes were used to communicate the essence of a bird in flight. The multiple triangles contribute diagonals to the composition that make it highly active. The two circles that define the head enable the viewer's eye to momentarily pause and focus on the form.

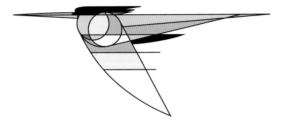

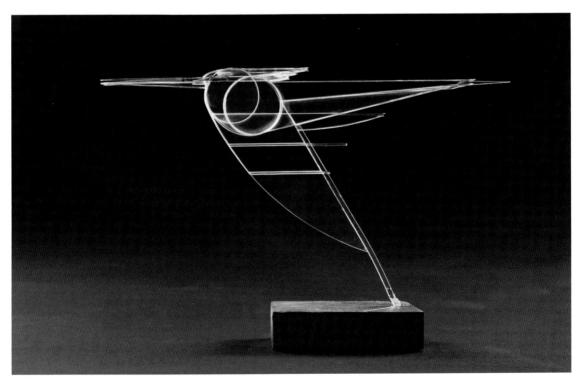

Kyle Snider

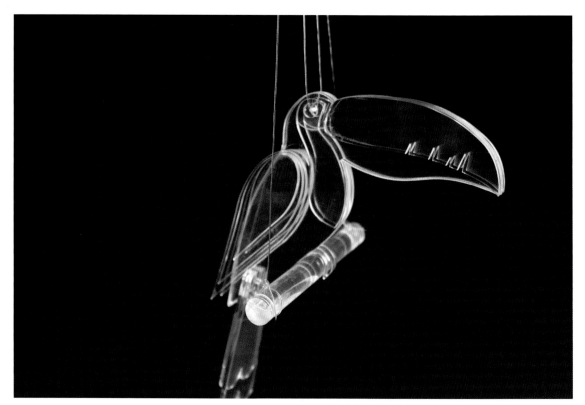

Stephen Moore

Initially, an acrylic-dowel perch was used to hang the toucan. However, balance was an issue, and additional strands of fishing line were used to hang in an upright position. Additional planes define changes in feather color on the throat and wings as well as the details in the beak.

The changes in color in the toucan are suggested by the planes of acrylic as the highlights move from the eye to the breast in a graceful arc. The triangular ridges in the beak contrast the curvilinear planes.

James Harris

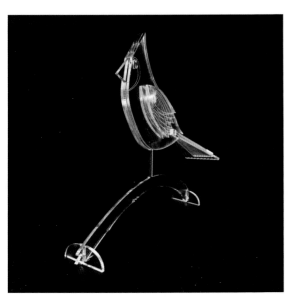

The design of the wings of the cardinal took advantage of vector scoring, which cuts a line only partway into the material and creates a minute valley that captures light in the clear acrylic. There are only two layers of acrylic in both the wings and tail, but they appear to have much more due to the repeated scored shapes. The arched stand allows the bird to be lifted from the surface and into the air.

The owl is posed in a classic frontal view. The bird is highly symmetric, which contrasts the asymmetric placement of the bird on the stand to the left of the vertical support. The extension of the craggy branch to the right beautifully balances the composition. The rhythm and repetition of the chest feathers provides a sense of movement as they direct the eye to move up and down the planes.

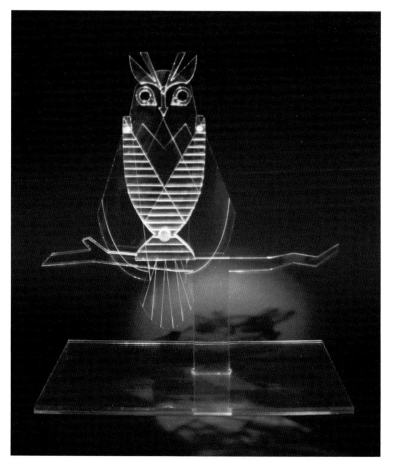

Lok Yiu Louise Fung

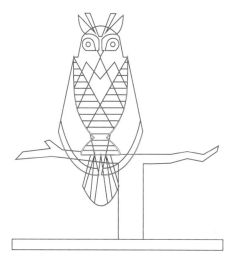

Tho ologanco of tho cardinal stems
from the contrast between the sinuous curves that travel down the face
and the straight lines of the wings
and back that travel down to the tail.
The triangular geometry of the head
and crest is repeated in the beak
and wings, which lends the model
cohesiveness. The bird stands on
the perch with only one foot, and
balance of the model is achieved by
the tail resting on the table surface.

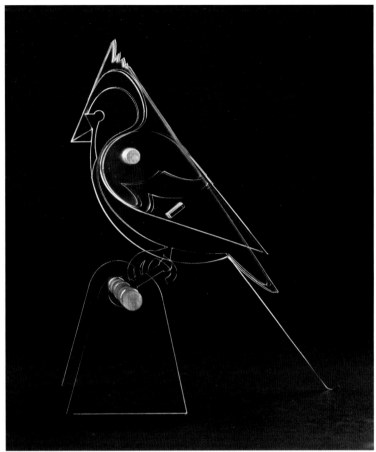

Michiru Morita

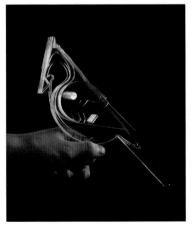

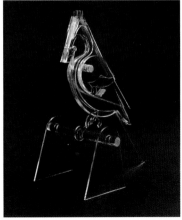

Poseable Bird

The skimmer is a small seabird that constantly scurries and searches for minute bits of food along the seashore. This skimmer is poseable due to the acrylic dowels attached to the legs and wings; the dowels also enable the planes to be rotated. A vector-score pattern on the triangular wings gives them a sense of animation, especially when rotated.

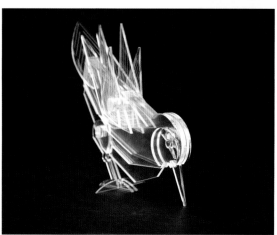

Jackson Dunson

Interlocking Plane Bird

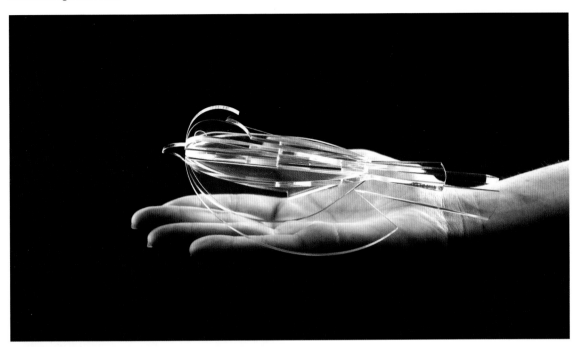

Martin Pholmann

Six interlocking planes define the three-dimensional volume of this bird and instills in it a sense of delicacy. Planes extend from the body to become the head, wings, and feet. Those same planes extend backward to form the tail. The head is defined by the beak, eye, and small crest at the top of the head.

Contributors

Without the contributions from my many students at Ringling College, this book would not exist. Students have been my collaborators in developing ideas, projects, and processes. It is an honor to be their teacher, and I am always inspired by their creativity.

Special thanks to my colleagues Jeff Bleitz and Kim Litch for their contributions of student work and for their advice and support. Finally, thanks to the professional artists, designers, and photographers who so generously contributed their beautiful work.

Index

DESIGN BRIEFS—essential texts on design

Also available in this series:

Designing for Social Change, Andrew Shea

Digital Design Theory, Helen Armstrong

D.I.Y Design It Yourself, Ellen Lupton

Elements of Design, Gail Greet Hannah

Form + Code in Design, Art, and Architecture,
Casey Reas, Chandler McWilliams, LUST

Geometry of Design, 2nd Edition, Kimberly Elam

Graphic Design Theory, Helen Armstrong

Graphic Design Thinking, Ellen Lupton

Grid Systems, Kimberly Elam

Indie Publishing, Ellen Lupton

Lettering & Type, Bruce Willen & Nolen Strals

Participate, Armstrong & Stojmirovic

Thinking with Type, 2nd edition, Ellen Lupton

Type on Screen, Ellen Lupton

Typographic Systems, Kimberly Elam

Visual Grammar, Christian Leborg

The Wayfinding Handbook, David Gibson